BUDDHISH

A GUIDE TO THE 20 MOST IMPORTANT BUDDHIST IDEAS FOR THE CURIOUS AND SKEPTICAL

C. PIERCE SALGUERO

Beacon Press,
BOSTON

BEACON PRESS
Boston, Massachusetts
www.beacon.org

Beacon Press books
are published under the auspices of
the Unitarian Universalist Association of Congregations.

25 24 23 22   8 7 6 5 4 3 2 1

This book is printed on acid-free paper that meets the uncoated paper
ANSI/NISO specifications for permanence as revised in 1992.

Text design and composition by Kim Arney

Library of Congress Cataloging-in-Publication Data
Name: Salguero, C. Pierce, author.
Title: Buddhish: a guide to the 20 most important Buddhist ideas
for the curious and skeptical / C. Pierce Salguero.
Description: Boston: Beacon Press, 2022. | Summary: "Finally, a balanced
and readable introduction to Buddhism for open minded readers who have
no interest in professing faith in a new religion or adopting
a new ideology"—Provided by publisher.
Identifiers: LCCN 2021047964 | ISBN 9780807064566 (trade paperback) |
ISBN 9780807064764 (ebook)
Subjects: LCSH: Buddhism. | Buddhism—Popular works.
Classification: LCC BQ4022 .S25 2022 | DDC 294.3—dc23
LC record available at https://lccn.loc.gov/2021047964

BUDDHISH

Attadipa viharatha

CONTENTS

NOTE ON
BUDDHIST LANGUAGES

A general book on Buddhism is complicated by the fact that there are many languages to navigate. In this book, I have defaulted to Sanskrit when I am speaking in a general way about Buddhist terminology. If there is a culturally specific reference, however, I default to the language from that culture instead. In a few cases, I've overridden these defaults and opted to use whatever term is most widely used in English-language literature instead. All of this is to facilitate the reader's ongoing research and exploration of these concepts.

While it goes against my scholarly instincts, I have removed all diacritical marks from the foreign languages used here. In the interests of readability, I have also used standard phonetic transcriptions for Tibetan.

All translations throughout the book are my own unless otherwise attributed.

INTRODUCTION

A re you curious about Buddhism? Wondering what the hubbub is all about but roll your eyes every time you try to read a book about it? Well, if so, relax. This is not your ordinary introduction to Buddhism. This is not a book that teaches you how to practice meditation, and it's not a self-help guide. There are none of the saccharine platitudes, high-minded moralizing, or dense pontification that you may have come to expect from a book on Buddhism. Nor is it a dry scholarly treatment of Buddhism filled with academic terminology and concepts. It is meant for open-minded or even skeptical readers who have no interest in professing faith in a new religion or adopting a new ideology.

This book presents a balanced introduction to twenty of the central principles of Buddhism, as I understand them and as I have experienced them. By the end of the book, you will have toured the Buddhist world and learned about how certain Buddhist ideas have been understood in China, Korea, Japan, Thailand, Tibet, and other cultures, including the West. You will know about some of the current trends in the academic study of Buddhism. You might even see how certain Buddhist ideas apply to your own situation and help to navigate challenges in your own life. What you won't get is indoctrination. I promise in these pages I will not try to convince you to practice Buddhism or to become Buddhist.

Who am I? Why should you trust me as your tour guide? Well, let me start by confessing that I am not Buddhist. I have no Asian heritage or family connections to Buddhism either. In fact, I come from a bilingual and transnational Latino family with roots in Colombia, Uruguay, Spain, England, and the United States. I spent my early childhood in Canada and Paraguay, and moved to the US during elementary school. There's a lot of Catholicism and Protestantism in my family tree, as well as some native Amerindian blood; yet when I was growing up, we never talked about religion at all. To be honest, I don't even remember the first time I heard of Buddhism, but I imagine it must have been when I was in high school, when I started to become interested in several Asian spiritual traditions. Yet, somehow, Buddhism sparked my interest most of all, and it drew me in.

In the thirty years since that interest first took root, I have developed a long-term relationship with Buddhism by experiencing it and engaging with it in many different ways. I can honestly say I have come to have an enormous amount of interest, respect, and affection for this tradition, and it has been a constant companion throughout basically all of my adult life.

Here in this book, I will share with you my own personal perspective on Buddhism. I will weave in anecdotes from when I spent the summer in a monastery in a rural temple in the rainforest of eastern Thailand. I will bring in insights from the five years that I was a serious practitioner of *vipassana* meditation and the decade or so I have spent living in various parts of Asia (including not only Thailand but also India and Taiwan). I will also draw a lot on my fifteen years of experience studying Buddhism as an academic, during which time I have read extensively about its history and even learned to read medieval Chinese so that I could understand certain Buddhist texts in their original language. I will reflect on both the ways that Buddhist ideas and practices have helped me to navigate my own life and the ways that I have seen it help others.

Despite this extensive background, I repeat, I am not Buddhist. I am not a meditation teacher or a model practitioner. When asked to identify my religion, I like to joke that I might be "Buddhish." I think Buddhism has had a lot to offer me, and I have cared about it for a long time, but I don't believe most of the stories, don't engage in most of the practices, and don't even agree with most of the philosophies. I have learned a lot from the tradition, but I have used my own judgment to evaluate what is useful and what is right for me. I have accepted some ideas and practices, but I have rejected many of the basic premises of the tradition. I am a student, friend, and fan of Buddhism but also a critic.

So, to be clear, what I am offering you here is a Buddhish book, not a Buddhist one. It is a Buddhish book. It is not a book written for Buddhists or for scholars of Buddhism. If you have an extensive background in Buddhism already, yet you insist on reading this book, then I assure you that you will find it objectionable. You'll say that it's oversimplified, that it's skewed, that it's idiosyncratic, and that it doesn't do justice to your own particular understanding of or approach to Buddhism. So, if that's you, please look elsewhere. This book is intended for people who are complete newcomers, who don't already have a strong view about Buddhism one way or the other, and who are curious to learn what it's all about in a lighthearted way without any doctrinal heavy lifting.

Why am I writing this book? Well, I think we need this kind of introduction to Buddhism. With mindfulness on the covers of magazines in the grocery store checkout lane and Dalai Lama memes all over the Internet, Buddhism is seemingly everywhere these days. Even so, it's difficult to find a good introduction that speaks to ordinary people. Bookstore shelves are piled high with how-tos written by monks and meditators who preach the virtues of devoting your life to Buddhist practices. On the other end of the shelf, there are thick academic tomes that detail the history and doctrine in mind-numbing detail (some of which I myself have written!). This book is intended to fill a niche between these extremes. If you are curious about Buddhism and are looking for an accessible introduction in plain English, if you are open-minded to learning about what Buddhists think and say but don't necessarily want to be pressured to commit yourself to adopting these convictions yourself, then this is a book for you.

Before we start, I would like to ask for something from you. Even if you don't know very much at all about Buddhism, I am sure that you already have some preconceptions. Just by virtue of being a literate person alive in the twenty-first century, you have, I am pretty certain, already absorbed certain stereotypes about it. You probably associate Buddhism with peace, with mental health, with friendliness, and with harmony. When I say "Buddhism," the first image that comes to mind is likely the smiling face of the Dalai Lama, a meditation teacher sitting on a cushion in lotus posture, or a golden Buddha statue from one Asian country or another. You may already have a feeling that Buddhism is a philosophy or a science of the mind or a lifestyle that attracts certain kinds of people. I am going to ask you to try to leave all of these preconceptions behind before you start reading. As I will demonstrate, a lot of these ideas are based on superficial or even wrongheaded notions of Buddhism. I am going to ask that you, as much as possible, try to start this book with a blank slate. In the words of the pioneering Zen teacher Shunryu Suzuki (1904–1971), do your best to bring a "beginner's mind" to this endeavor. Please let these pages take you on a journey to an unfamiliar land, and allow yourself to be surprised and expanded by the new sights you find there.

This journey will introduce you, in twenty brief chapters, to what I think are the twenty most important ideas from the Buddhist tradition. Each chapter includes an introduction to the idea in plain English, based on my own understanding and experience. It may also include a discussion of how this concept has been understood or applied by practicing Buddhists in certain times and places, or how it has been understood by scholars of Buddhist studies (of course, always using accessible terms), or how it played a role in an anecdote from my past, or how it can be illustrated by a thought experiment or an everyday situation.

These chapters build upon one another, so it is a good idea to read them in order the first time. You will see that there's a general arc to the book: The first half largely focuses on Buddhism's promise that we can be liberated from suffering if we learn to see the truth about what's real and what's not. The second half focuses on the many ways that Buddhism has been practiced in the everyday world. While I have limited the use of technical Buddhist terminology, throughout the book I have provided some key Buddhist terms in *italics* on first reference, so that you can look them up on Wikipedia or another encyclopedia for further study. I mention books and other resources throughout these pages, but at the very end, I also have provided a list of some of my favorites, if you are interested in digging even deeper into the ideas presented here.

With those preliminaries aside, as your guide, let me be the first to welcome you to this brand-new world! As you turn the page, you will be meeting a rich tradition with lots of things to say about what reality is like and how we should live life. Buddhism has a deep history of cultural diversity, and many beautiful stories and inspirational sentiments. Along the way, I'll also point out some of the biases and contradictions. My intention isn't to judge Buddhism's track record one way or the other but rather to give you an introduction to the most salient features of the tradition, to give you the lay of the land—including the good, the bad, and the ugly—and to invite you to decide for yourself what to think about it all. If that sounds good to you, hop on board this tour bus, and let's get started!

1

AWAKENING

Legend has it that once in a while a truly remarkable person is born who can see the ultimate truth of reality the way that no one else can and who can teach others to see it as well. The starting point for our exploration of Buddhist ideas is the story told about the life of one such person. If you are unfamiliar with the basic outline of the story of the Buddha, let me quickly recap for you how it is told in the ancient text, *Acts of the Buddha* (*Buddhacarita*):

Siddhartha Gautama, the person who would eventually become the Buddha, is born in extraordinary circumstances to the king and queen of a small kingdom based at Kapilavastu, northeastern India, somewhere in the middle of the first millennium BCE. There are various omens and miracles that accompany his birth—including the fact that he is born from his mother's side without any pain and that he immediately takes seven steps and declares out loud that this is his last rebirth. Also, there are some remarkable features to the baby's body, including his golden-hued skin and the wheel marks on his hands and feet. To interpret these signs, a soothsayer is called in. The wise old man declares that the boy has a most auspicious destiny, predicting that he will either become a world-ruling monarch or a fully Awakened spiritual leader.

The king, as one might imagine, desires the former rather than the latter for his progeny. So he hatches a plan to ensconce his son within the palace and to surround him with all of the wealth and sensual pleasures one could imagine. His idea is that if the boy experiences a life of luxury, he will never give rise to the kind of yearning or discontent that leads one to ask serious spiritual or religious questions. So Siddhartha grows up pampered, surrounded by beauty, given all the delicacies his heart desires, and entertained by lovely maidens and heavenly music.

The king's plan goes well enough for a while. Siddhartha grows up, gets married, has a son, and seems to be on track to inherit his father's throne. However, the crown prince cannot avoid a persistent nagging feeling that this is not the life for him, that there is more to life than wealth and pleasure. Eventually, Siddhartha repeatedly sneaks out of the palace where he has been sequestered, and it is beyond the palace gates that he comes in contact for the first time with the real world.

On his journeys outside the palace, he sees four things that shake him to his core. First, he runs into an elderly man, which he has never seen before, and which causes him to realize that all human beings inevitably will grow old and suffer the discomforts of aging. Next, he sees a sick man, which causes him to realize that no one can avoid the experience of bodily pain and illness. Third, he encounters a corpse, whereupon he realizes that all of us eventually will die. Finally, he comes across a renunciate—a spiritual seeker, generically called *sramana* in India—who has given up the worldly life in order to pursue spiritual or religious goals. Amazed by the renunciate's demeanor and wisdom, Siddhartha comes to realize that there is an alternative way of being in the world other than the sheltered life he has known, a way which promises a path to a place beyond old age, sickness, and death.

Now consumed by the idea of becoming a spiritual seeker himself, Siddhartha decides to run away from home to live in the forest. One night, while his family is fast asleep, he creeps out of the palace.

His escape is facilitated by a number of supernatural beings who are plotting to help him. These angel-like creatures (generically referred to as *devas*) put a sleeping spell on the guards and residents of the palace, and carry Siddhartha's horse through the air so the sound of its hooves does not disturb anyone's slumber.

Upon his arrival in the forest, Siddhartha studies with a wide range of teachers and spiritual guides who, like him, have renounced the worldly life. (Actually, from what we know about ancient Indian religious culture, this form of renunciation seems to have been fairly widespread at the time. All sorts of philosophers, sages, and yogis are said to have been practicing and teaching one another in the forest.) Siddhartha quickly excels at the techniques the forest masters are teaching their followers, but he finds himself continually dissatisfied with these practices. He doubts that anything he is learning actually holds the key to liberation from the human condition. He even goes so far as to practice extreme forms of asceticism, such as starving himself nearly to death in order to forcibly achieve higher states of consciousness, but he soon realizes that this too is a dead-end path.

Finally, Siddhartha decides to break off from the rest of the spiritual seekers, and he sets out to forge his own path. Taking a seat under a large *bodhi* tree (Latin name: *Ficus religiosa*), he makes a solemn vow not to move from that posture until he has attained the realization he seeks. At this point in the story, various forces of evil, personified as the demon Mara and his children, attempt to break his resolve. They try to scare or seduce him away from pursuing his goal, but Siddhartha persists. Using meditation skills he has acquired from various past experiences, he enters a series of deep trancelike states.

Over the course of the night, a series of insights comes to Siddhartha while he is meditating. He attains a kind of omniscient understanding of the way the human mind and body work. He becomes aware of all of his previous lives and of the intricate workings of karma. Eventually, he reaches a state of wisdom beyond the comprehension of ordinary people—a state that can only be described as perfection. Having this realization ensures he will never be reborn again. As he puts it, he has gone to "the farther shore of birth and death." He has discovered a timeless truth about the universe and has reached the zenith of our human potential. When someone later asks him if he is a god, an angel, a demon, or a human being, he denies all of those options and states simply that he has become a Buddha, which literally means an Awakened One.

The story continues. Though the Buddha is initially reluctant to teach, soon after his Awakening he begins taking on disciples. These individuals, collectively called the *sangha* or "the community," are like him in that they have abandoned their worldly lives and social positions in order to become spiritual seekers, or renunciates. The Buddha and his disciples take to wandering through the countryside, through villages, and through cities spreading the Buddha's teachings throughout northeastern India. Many stories are told about the teachings and activities of the Buddha and the sangha over the remainder of his life.

Decades later, at the ripe old age of eighty, the Buddha passes away from food poisoning (of all things!) while surrounded by his many disciples and devoted lay supporters. After his death, his closest followers gathered together stories about the master and accounts of what he had taught over his life. These narratives, which were memorized and passed down orally among his followers, eventually become the Buddhist scriptures (*sutras*) that we have today. (This is why most Buddhist scriptures start with the unusual line "This is what I heard . . ." They are understood to be spoken in the voice of one of the Buddha's disciples—usually his closest student, Ananda— as they recall what they heard the Buddha say.)

So that's the story of the Buddha and the origins of Buddhism. What are we to make of it?

Before I address that question, I first want to acknowledge that for most Buddhists throughout history, this narrative has been understood as a literal account whose facticity is beyond dispute. Even most modern Buddhists believe that the story is largely true, though they acknowledge that certain details (such as talking babies, flying horses, and helpful angels, for example) are fictional embellishments. On the other hand, scholars, who approach this story from a historical rather than a devotional perspective, have understood the tale to be mostly or even wholly mythological.

Why do scholars have this view? Well, first, they point out that there are several different versions of this biography of the Buddha. Importantly, none of these accounts dates as far back as the period when the Buddha is said to have lived, around the fifth or sixth century BCE. These various renditions of the story have been handed down by different Buddhist traditions in the Sanskrit, Pali, Chinese, and Tibetan languages (among others), and they differ from one another on many points. If there was once a core narrative shared by these traditions, it is quite clear that by the time the texts we have today were written down, the story had been transformed, elaborated, and reinterpreted over centuries of oral telling and retelling.

The scholars of early Buddhism most sympathetic to religious claims about a "historical Buddha" (such as the retired Oxford University professor Richard F. Gombrich, author of many books on the subject) have spent their careers trying to peel back the more obviously mythological layers in order to establish evidence of a real-life individual who lived and died in ancient northeastern India. Most historians who have embarked on this endeavor concur that, if such a person actually lived, he likely would have done so around a century or two later than the traditional dating. They believe he would probably have lived in the kingdom of Magadha, in modern-day Bihar Province in eastern India. As much as they have tried to uncover more details about him, however, very little else can be definitively said about the historical figure behind the founding of Buddhism.

I will lay my cards on the table as a skeptic and say that I think it is important to base our understanding of history on concrete evidence. To put it bluntly: there is no conclusive evidence whatsoever that the details of the story related above—even the basic plotline of a prince who abandons his position to become a spiritual seeker—is historically true. The fact that someone authored a narrative about the Buddha several hundred years after his lifetime is not even proof that he was a real person. As a historian with a high standard of evidence, I would need to see corroborating documentary evidence from the Buddha's lifetime, preferably from outside of the Buddhist tradition, in order to accept the story of the Buddha's life as anything other than a myth.

At the same time, I don't think that the historical veracity of the life of the Buddha is the most relevant issue. Just because a story is a myth does not mean it is unimportant. The story of the Buddha's life is a classic of world literature precisely because it is a masterpiece that has inspired hundreds of millions of people over the centuries. It is one of those archetypal narratives—like the life of Jesus, or the *Odyssey*, or even *Star Wars*—that speaks to universal concerns. The story of the Buddha is a perfectly constructed myth, the epitome of both the genres of coming-of-age and the hero's quest. For this reason, I think that every modern educated person should be familiar with it and that anyone and everyone can draw inspiration from it.

As a myth, the biography of the Buddha is both heartbreaking and uplifting. Who among us can't relate to the king in the story, wanting desperately to protect our children from experiencing the inevitable pain and suffering of the real world? And who among us hasn't also been the child in the story, growing up happily sheltered only to inevitably lose our innocence? Who among us hasn't had to confront the brutal realities of old age, illness, and death, and longed for a way to escape these inevitabilities? Being exposed to these painful truths for the first time inspires Siddhartha to reflect on the meaning of his life and to set out on his own path. Who among us hasn't also longed for the deeper meaning, self-realization, and self-transformation that Siddhartha achieves?

It's this last idea especially, the possibility of following in the Buddha's footsteps and becoming Awakened ourselves, that I want to draw attention to. This is the first concept on our list of the most powerful Buddhist ideas. All forms of Buddhism that I know of share this basic belief. They may express it or interpret it differently, but they all agree that human beings have an innate ability to become Awakened. To wake up from our ordinary way of seeing the world. To discover a truth that will completely shift our perspective. To enter a new state of consciousness and a new state of being.

Ultimately, because this book is Buddhish and not Buddhist, you'll have to decide for yourself whether or not this idea is inspirational and what it might mean in your own life. Is this kind of Awakening really possible? Are we really sleeping through our lives? How would being Awakened change us? How would it feel to see the world like the Buddha? There are so many questions, and we'll address many of them in the pages to come.

2

SUFFERING

In the story of the Buddha's life, his quest for Awakening is inspired by his encounters with *duhkha* (rhymes with "hookah"). This Buddhist concept is often translated into English simply as "suffering," but the word takes on a wider range of meanings in different contexts. Duhkha can describe the physical pains that one experiences in old age, illness, and death, but the same word may instead refer to emotions like sadness, depression, or mental anguish. It also may refer to a general feeling of dissatisfaction, a sense that things aren't quite right or that our purpose in life is something more than what we're currently doing. Duhkha also can refer to the feeling of regret when we are prevented from experiencing pleasure, or the sense of loss when events that we are enjoying come to an end. This one word thus refers to the entire range of negative and dissatisfactory human experiences, the whole spectrum of emotional and physical experiences that we all wish to avoid.

Buddhism's basic position on duhkha, which is made clear in countless Buddhist texts from different traditions, is that these kinds of negative states are an inescapable part of life for all human beings. Buddhist doctrine asks us to accept the fact that life has a propensity to go awry. No matter what we do, we are subject to unfortunate events beyond our control. By virtue of being born, we are trapped by the inevitability of duhkha: we simply must experience pain, discomfort, dissatisfaction, and uncertainty.

Buddhism's teachings on the inevitability of suffering have led a lot of people to conclude that it is deeply pessimistic. I agree, but I also think that this sense of pessimism is one of Buddhism's most important insights. Of course, taking this idea too far may lead to nihilism, to overwhelming depression, or to the inability to find meaning or joy in anything at all. However, as with the other concepts introduced throughout this book, if you approach duhkha as a tool to think with rather than as an ideology to subscribe to, I do think that it can be quite useful.

Accepting the inevitability of duhkha can, for example, dissuade us from blindly trusting in someone else. Taking this concept seriously means accepting that no gurus, priests, politicians, family members, or heroes are going to arrive on the scene and permanently erase our pain and discomfort. It is an antidote for the kind of magical thinking that says, "If only I had the right partner, spouse, etc., then I wouldn't be so lonely," or "If only I had a different kind of boss, officemate, etc., then I wouldn't dislike my job." Likewise with material possessions or worldly attainments: a bigger house, newer car, or better paying job might contribute to my material comfort, but they will not prevent me from experiencing duhkha.

In fact, there will always be a constant flow of duhkha in my life. As soon as I solve one problem, I am guaranteed another source of dissatisfaction. For example, I might buy that new car today, but will that prevent my toilet from overflowing or my tooth from falling out tomorrow? Alas, even pleasant experiences inevitably lead to duhkha, either because the experience itself ends or because the pleasure I derive from it eventually peters out. For example, while the first scoop of ice cream tastes great, how do we feel about the third? The tenth? If you eat even your favorite food to excess, it eventually becomes disgusting.

A certain amount of pessimism can also be a corrective to our propensity to put a positive spin on events. The concept of duhkha teaches us to be skeptical of platitudes such as "The arc of history bends toward justice" or "If you put good vibes out into the world, good things will happen to you." While it might be appropriate to tell ourselves these comforting things in certain situations, duhkha asks us to accept the cold, hard facts that injustice persists around the world and that bad things happen to the innocent all the time. Duhkha asks us to accept that there is no god watching out for us from on high who is protecting us from misfortune, no lucky coin we can rub to ensure our safety or success.

Duhkha was on my mind in 2004 when an earthquake with a magnitude of at least 9.1 struck off the coast of the Indonesian island of Sumatra. The quake produced tsunami waves up to one hundred feet high, causing damage as far away as Sri Lanka, India, and the east coast of Africa, and wreaking complete devastation in certain parts of Southeast Asia. The US Geological Survey reported that the death toll was about 228,000, and UNICEF estimated on its website that nearly one-third of the dead were children. According to the Asian Disaster Preparedness Center, the event caused somewhere in the neighborhood of $10 billion in damage in some of the poorest areas of the globe. This was a tragedy of monumental proportions.

Although I was in the United States attending graduate school at the time, I had spent several years living in Thailand and knew many people who had been directly affected. Shortly after the tsunami, I traveled to the southwestern coast in order to participate in a relief project focused on affected children. Both while I was on the scene in Thailand and when I read reports of the disaster in the global press coverage during that time, I kept hearing religious leaders, government officials, and ordinary people trying to make sense of the devastation. One question many people tried to answer was why this had happened. Was it the result of some collective bad karma in the region? A wrathful divine punishment for some sin or another?

Many Thai people I met in the affected region told me stories about how they personally were saved from the tsunami—because they possessed a certain lucky amulet, for example, or practiced a particular protective ritual or had particularly good karma. Some Western people working with Christian charity groups said they thought this was a test of faith in God. Many Thais and Westerners, regardless of their faith, tried to find a silver lining in the event. They pointed to examples of charity, generosity, and cooperation that spontaneously emerged in the aftermath as evidence that lessons could be learned even in the most difficult times.

Such attempts to find the reasons for or the meaning behind terrible events are a normal human response to any catastrophe. Humans are meaning-making animals; we want to know why things happen, and we are uncomfortable with arbitrariness. This is especially true with regard to painful events, large and small. When faced with such horrors, we ask, "Why me?" or "Why us?" or "Why this?" or "Why now?" We try to console ourselves that things happen for a reason. We appeal to all sorts of magical tools, gods, divination practices, and speculations to try to give meaning to the senseless randomness.

However, if we rigorously applied the lesson of duhkha, the acceptance of the inevitability of suffering, to a situation like the 2004 tsunami, it would mean abandoning this line of thought altogether. It would mean accepting that horrific things happen to us for no reason whatsoever—or at least for no discernable reason that we would ever be able to figure out and therefore is useless to try to fathom. It would mean surrendering to the fact that living human beings will experience many forms of suffering, both major and minor, over the course of our lives. This is not because pain and suffering is planned by the gods or by the Fates but simply because it is an inevitable part of the human experience. Accepting duhkha means that we have to give up the belief that we can pray away tsunamis and the fantasy that there will come a time when everything is perfect.

This kind of radical acceptance of duhkha is a central concept in Buddhism. It is, in fact, the first of the so-called Four Noble Truths. Introduced in the *Discourse on the Turning of the Wheel of Dharma* (*Dhammacakkappavattana Sutta*), which is said to be the Buddha's very first sermon, this doctrine represents his most basic teaching.

(This text is part of the *Tripitaka*, in Pali meaning "three baskets," the complete collection of Buddhist scriptures.) According to the Buddha, it is only when we accept that duhkha is inevitable for all human beings as a natural part of our lives that we can begin to work toward Awakening and eventually liberate ourselves from all suffering.

Hold on a sec. If duhkha is the inescapable nature of human existence, isn't it paradoxical to say that full Awakening is a state of permanent and total liberation from suffering? To make sense of this, it is important to understand that the Buddha is not promising that human beings can reach a state in which they will no longer experience any catastrophes, disasters, or other unpleasant experiences. He is not promising that you will never physically age, become physically ill, or physically die. He is not promising that your nerve endings will stop sending pain signals to your brain when you stub your toe. These experiences remain inevitable and cannot be avoided by any living human being—even those who are fully Awakened.

The claim is not that the Four Noble Truths are going to change the realities around us but rather that they will change the way that we experience those realities. The doctrine offers us a means whereby we might experience those calamities and disasters without being adversely affected psychologically. To weather unpleasant situations and conditions without experiencing them negatively. As many Buddhist teachers have put it, we can learn to separate pain from suffering—that is, to feel the nerve endings fire when we are hurt, but to meet them with acceptance and equanimity without adding our own mental reactions, anxiety, and woe on top of them.

The first step in that process, we are told, is to accept the presence of duhkha. This means acknowledging large-scale pain and discomfort, but it also means acknowledging all minor forms of duhkha in our present situation as well. It means embracing the imperfection of life and the inevitability of dissatisfaction.

Building on this first Noble Truth, the second Noble Truth tells us that the cause of our dissatisfaction and unpleasantness is actually within our own minds. Our duhkha is being caused by our own insatiable wanting. We are constantly wanting to change a situation or wanting things to remain the same or wanting to have certain objects or wanting to not have other objects, and all of this wanting is preventing us from being okay with how things actually are in any given moment.

From this insight follows the third Noble Truth, which says that if we were able to just be okay with the present moment, then we would logically become free from our dissatisfaction.

But how to do that? The fourth Noble Truth tells us that becoming free is possible by following the Buddha's Eightfold Noble Path. I'll come back to this idea in the next chapter, but for now, let's just say that this is the Buddha's prescription for how to think, how to live, how to practice, and how to meditate in order to overcome wanting and to defeat duhkha once and for all.

If the Four Noble Truths are the Buddha's solution to humankind's ultimate malady, I think it is a bitter pill he's asking us to swallow. For milder forms of dissatisfaction, it seems straightforward enough. I'm sitting on the airplane on a long flight, and my legs are getting sore. We're encountering turbulence, and the seatbelt light is on, so I can't get up to stretch. I really am wanting to change this situation to be more comfortable, but what choices do I have? Should I get angry at someone? Should I get anxious, counting the minutes and seconds till I can stand up? Should I fill up my body with alcohol or pain pills to try to escape my misery? Or should I figure out some way to curb my desire for change and just sit with the pain? The Buddha says the latter is the correct choice, and he promises that if I accept the unpleasant sensations in my body, as they are, without wanting them to be different, then they may not go away, but I won't experience them as suffering.

Fair enough. But what about more severe forms of suffering? Imagine a more devastating scenario: The tsunami hits, your community is in shambles, your home is destroyed, and your friends and family are killed. You are distraught, filled with pain and anguish. What can you do? Who do you turn to? What tools for coping does the Buddha have to offer you in this moment of crisis? Well, the doctrine of the

Four Noble Truths simply tells you to stop wanting things to be different; it tells you that you need to learn to just sit with the pain.

In case you think I'm exaggerating with this last example, there's a famous story from the *Tripitaka* about a woman named Kisa Gotami who visits the Buddha in a state of desperation because her child has just died. She asks him for a remedy to bring her son back to life. The Buddha replies that he will help her, but first she must go and fetch a mustard seed from a family that has never experienced any death. Thinking that the Buddha is going to do some kind of healing ritual, Kisa Gotami excitedly sets out on this quest. But she soon finds that every family has experienced death and that no such mustard seed exists. Realizing that the experience of death is universal snaps her out of her desperate grief, and she is so inspired by this insight that she becomes a nun in the Buddha's monastic order. The moral of the story, of course, is that suffering is inescapable and universal. That even when facing the ultimate personal nightmare, we all need to stop being in denial and find a way to sit with the duhkha.

What do you think? Is this story helpful? Is this concept of simply accepting duhkha useful? Sure, the pill is bitter, but is it good medicine? Can it help us to see things more objectively? Can it provide some kind of insight into the nature of human experience? As we go forward, you'll see that I'm not going to answer those kinds of questions for you in this book. I'm not going to tell you that this is how you *should* think. I'm just going to lay out the ideas for you and let you decide what to do with them yourself. What I do want to point out is that millions of Buddhists have for centuries found solace in this doctrine and have put the Four Noble Truths into practice in their own lives in order to deal with all varieties of duhkha, big and small.

Since we're being Buddhish and not Buddhist, don't worry if this message doesn't resonate with you. Maybe it never will, but we've got a long way to go before you decide what you think about Buddhism, and there's plenty more to talk about.

3

PATH

I'm going to be honest with you: I'm not a fan of lists. You probably won't believe me, since I've already introduced the Four Truths in the previous chapter, and in this one we're going to talk about the Eightfold Path. But, I've picked up many introductory books on Buddhism that consist of lists upon lists, and I've come to think that this is probably the most boring way you could possibly learn about the tradition.

However, Buddhists seem to love lists. I'm sure this is related to the way that knowledge was carried orally for centuries before it was written down, as it's much easier to remember things in list form. List-making is probably also how people expected knowledge to be presented in India before the advent of writing. I bet it's no accident that the Eightfold Noble Path of Buddhism is parallel to the eightfold model of yoga and the eightfold disciplines of medicine that also developed in ancient India. (All of these systems use the word *ashtanga*, which means "eightfold" or "eight-limbed" in Sanskrit.)

That being said, in this book, I promise we will not dwell on lists. I will quickly enumerate the eight aspects of the Eightfold Noble Path here and then move on to what I think are the more interesting underlying considerations.

As mentioned in the previous chapter, the Eightfold Noble Path is the Buddha's prescription for overcoming duhkha. Remember, it's his contention that suffering and dissatisfaction are caused by our constantly wanting things, by not accepting the way things are from moment to moment. So this is the Buddha's plan for us to master our own mental processes in order to do away with that wanting. According to the *Analysis of the Path* (*Maggavibhanga Sutta*), a very influential text that introduces the model, the eight aspects of the Path are as follows:

1. Right view: We begin by accepting the postulates laid out in the Four Noble Truths, in order to gain proper understanding of the mission before us.
2. Right intention: We then strongly commit ourselves to Awakening. Usually, this aspect also involves a commitment to avoid dwelling in anger or committing acts of violence.
3. Right speech: We vow to avoid telling lies, using divisive or abusive speech, and engaging in "idle chatter."
4. Right action: We vow to avoid killing, stealing, and sexual misconduct. (The latter is defined differently whether you're a celibate monk or a married householder and is frequently updated to reflect local cultural norms.)
5. Right livelihood: We resolve to make a living in an ethically sound way that is free from dishonesty.
6. Right effort: We make efforts to maintain the "skillful" qualities we have already and to cultivate new ones. We also try to overcome the "unskillful" qualities we have already and to avoid taking on new ones. Skillful and unskillful qualities refer to states of mind and behavioral patterns that either help or hinder one's progress on the Path.
7. Right mindfulness: We reflect on the body and its sensations and the mind and its qualities. This practice is usually described in English as "meditation" and is a topic I'll have a lot more to say about in future chapters.

8. Right concentration: Through deeper practice of focused
meditation, we learn to produce certain states of intense concentration, which facilitate our realization of Awakening.

These eight aspects are presented in a different order or given
different interpretations in different Buddhist traditions. One common way of talking about them is to divide them up into the "three
trainings": wisdom (steps 1–2 on the above list), morality (steps 3–5),
and mental cultivation (steps 6–8).

Any way you slice them up, I think there are two larger principles
behind the Eightfold Noble Path that are important to discuss. These
are so fundamental to Buddhism that they almost go without saying.
They represent not only the foundations of this particular teaching
but also some key points that distinguish Buddhism from other traditions. These points are (1) the promise of human perfectibility and
(2) the necessity of individual practice.

Let's take these one at a time. First, the notion of human perfectibility. Depending on your own personal orientation, this may seem
perfectly natural to you, or it might seem slightly utopian, or it might
even seem downright delusional. Take a moment to think about it
before moving forward: Are people incapable of changing who they
fundamentally are? Are our personality traits and mental patterns essentially fixed once we reach adulthood? Is human nature essentially
bad? Are we slaves to our animal nature, perhaps controllable with
carrots and sticks but at the end of the day simply out for ourselves? Is
it hubris to think that any human might know what the reality of the
universe is? That any human might see and know the ultimate truth?

If you answered yes to any of those questions, most forms of Buddhism disagree with you. The Eightfold Noble Path is, at its core, a
doctrine based on the idea that human beings are malleable. That no
matter what your age, no matter what your biographical history, no
matter what your characteristics, you can always become a wiser, more
enlightened person. This is an optimistic and, yes, maybe even a utopian idea. But, in broad strokes, modern neuroscience and psychology

agree that the human brain and personality are not fixed. Current research on neuroplasticity is demonstrating that new neurons are formed throughout our lives and that new connections are forged even when elderly people engage with new forms of art, exercise, learning, and other practices. Meanwhile, the field of developmental psychology is showing that higher stages of cognitive development are attainable by adults as they continue to expand their ability to think and feel and that some of these domains only open up when we're well into adulthood.

What makes Buddhism different from the science of the brain or the psychology of adult development is that it promises not to merely improve your life but to lead you to the very pinnacle of human achievement. If you learned to play the piano as an older adult, a neuroscientist might say that you did something that is good for your mental health, and possibly your physical health as well. She might even agree it's important to become more well-rounded or to expand your horizons, but she wouldn't say you are becoming "perfected." Do you believe in perfectibility? Do you believe that there is even such a thing as a perfect human? Well, the Eightfold Noble Path makes precisely this claim about the skills it teaches. This is the Path to Perfection, the Path to becoming a Noble One. In Sanskrit, the term *arya-ashtanga-marga*—the Noble Eightfold Path or the Eightfold Path of the Noble Ones—is not referring to a hereditary aristocracy or anything like that. Rather, the word "noble" in this context indicates that this particular Path leads toward higher and higher states of human development, making you a better and better person and culminating ultimately in the full perfection of Awakening.

If perfectibility is the first of the main principles behind the Path, the second is the need for each of us to practice it individually. The Buddha laid out the Path, but we each need to take up the practices and make our own progress.

This emphasis on practice is such a core feature of Buddhism that it is easy to overlook. But it is a crucial aspect that separates Buddhism from other traditions. For example, certain forms of Christianity characterize humans as fallen creatures, sinful and in need of redemption. Their doctrine is based on the belief that only through God's grace can anyone attain salvation. In many forms of Christianity and also in Islam, it would be lunacy or even blasphemy to think that you can take matters into your own hands and to do God's work yourself. Other schools of thought, such as the ancient Chinese tradition of Daoism (often spelled "Taoism"), value non-action above all. For example, in early Daoist treatises such as the *Daode Jing* and the *Zhuangzi* (also spelled *Tao Te Ching* and *Chuang Tzu*), striving to improve oneself is described as useless and laughable. Buddhism, in contrast, is a program of self-development, self-improvement, and self-perfection. And the key to moving forward in that direction is to diligently keep up your practice.

Buddhist philosophers, meditation teachers, and intellectuals over the centuries have focused a lot of attention on the question of exactly how to practice, and they have developed elaborate maps of the "progress of insight." Influential historical Buddhist writings in this vein include titles such as *The Path of Freedom* (*Vimuttimaga*), *The Path of Purification* (*Visuddhimaga*), and the *Treatise on the Levels of Spiritual Practitioners* (*Yogacarabhumi Sastra*), all written by famous Buddhist monks in the first millennium CE. In Tibet, there are many competing descriptions of the stages of the Path (called *lamrim* in Tibetan). All of these works map out the types of mental, physical, and emotional phenomena that one experiences in deep meditation practice and describe how to move along the Path in a sequential way.

This traditional literature can be quite dense and difficult to read, but in modern times, detailed instructions on Buddhist meditation have become more accessible than ever before. Books still continue to be published that lay out step-by-step instructions on how to traverse the Path. Some popular contemporary guides written by Western teachers with very different approaches and tones are *A Path with Heart* by Jack Kornfield, *Practicing the Jhanas* by Stephen Snyder and Tina Rasmussen, and *Mastering the Core Teachings of the Buddha* by Daniel M. Ingram. If the reliability and structure of maps, charts, and lists are attractive to you; if an outline of the different levels of attainments that are possible and clear instructions on how to achieve these stages seems helpful; or if you find yourself getting into difficult territory while practicing meditation and could use some signposts to get back on track—then this systematic and organized Path-mapping literature may have much to offer you.

Currently, meditation apps are also a popular way to get step-by-step guidance, and there are many on the market. The introductory series of meditations in the app *Waking Up*, created by the neuroscientist, meditator, and political commentator Sam Harris, is my favorite to use in my classes on Buddhism. There are also social media groups, discussion forums, and other online venues where practitioners are able to connect with one another. Whereas in previous eras it was taboo to talk openly about meditation experiences in any detail, these days many people gladly share their observations about the stages of the Path and help keep each other on track. (There is also a dark side to this kind of social interaction, however, as it can easily devolve into people arguing, bragging, and competing with one another.)

If you enter into this arena, you should know that the specific instructions and stages differ according to what model of the Path any particular group has mapped out. Although you may find some similarities between these different books, apps, and communities, they are never fully compatible with one another. Thus, it makes sense to shop around a bit first before committing to one or another model of practice.

You should also know that, while meditation is central to many Buddhist traditions, there are other forms of Buddhism with completely different takes on Awakening. We'll discuss these in more detail later in this book. For the moment, let's just say that while most forms of Buddhism place emphasis on meditation, there are some very important exceptions, including several schools we'll discuss in chapter 14 that believe it's impossible for us deluded people to become Awakened without the direct intervention of divine grace! One of the most confusing things for newcomers to wrap their minds around is the fact that there are so many different types of Buddhism that have developed over time, not to mention new ones that continue to emerge today, many of them with contradictory teachings.

Committed Buddhists today argue over which of these various competing perspectives is correct, and the debates can get heated. But we don't need to take sides in those debates here. Since we're Buddhish, not Buddhist, we can appreciate that Buddhism is a complex and multifaceted tradition, and we can understand how diverse approaches make this tradition richer as a whole. I think that, for us, it's less helpful to think of Buddhism as a single Path that needs to be embraced in its totality. Instead, we can start thinking of it as a vast collection of ideas and tools for human development that are useful to examine and consider one by one. We can then use our own discrimination to decide what, if anything, in this toolbox might work for us.

4

KARMA

Truth be told, it's actually a small minority of Buddhists who take up hardcore meditation practice in order to make a serious push forward on the Path to Awakening. For the vast majority of Buddhists, practice is much simpler, usually not even involving all of the eight aspects of the Eightfold Path. Most Buddhists, historically and today, have not seen Awakening as a terribly urgent matter because of their belief in karma.

Karma is one of the most important Buddhist ideas we'll explore in this book. Though modern Western Buddhists often don't believe in rebirth, this is an essential component of virtually all forms of Buddhism that have existed in history. The idea of rebirth has played a huge role in shaping practices around death, birth, and other aspects of life in Asia, and it also directly affects how Buddhists approach their practice. Most Buddhists view their quest for perfection taking place not within one lifetime but instead across centuries and millennia as they are reborn into different bodies. (The Buddha himself is said to have pursued perfection across countless lifetimes, and there is a whole category of Buddhist literature called *jataka* tales, consisting of fables about the Buddha's previous lives.)

According to the mainstream Buddhist worldview, all of us are constantly being born again and again into different bodies in an endless cycle called *samsara*. Most Buddhist traditions sketch out the different "destinations" that you can be reborn into that include not only human lifeforms but also animals and various levels of ethereal or spiritual beings. Being an animal is considered a worse rebirth than being human, a ghost is even worse, and the very worst is a being who is trapped in the subterranean hells undergoing constant torment. Better rebirths than humans include various classes of spirits or gods who have greater and greater (although never omnipotent) powers. In the Buddhist imagination, all "sentient beings"—meaning humans, the entire animal kingdom, plus all the spirits mentioned above—are constantly being born and dying, perpetually moving up and down the ladder of destinations based on the karma they accumulate through their actions over these lifetimes.

In Sanskrit, the word *karma* basically just means "action," but it implies both actions that you take and the eventual reactions to or effects of those actions down the road as well, both in this life and the next. In the most general terms, bad actions will inevitably result in worse outcomes and worse rebirths. The quality of these outcomes often has a direct relationship with the actions committed, so that, for example, greedy people in one life become poor in the next, or violent people in one life become victims of crime in the next. On the plus side, however, even if one makes only a small amount of progress on the Path toward perfection in any particular lifetime, that positively contributes to one's overall trajectory toward Awakening.

There is no birth destination anywhere across the universe that is isolated from the effects of karma. The gods may live for a very long time, but even they are subject to karma, eventually dying and returning to another body. Thus, although we might find some temporary enjoyment here or there when we happen to attain a better rebirth for a time, on the grand cosmic scale, samsara is by definition a cycle of suffering. The human life, located in the middle of the spectrum of possible rebirth destinations, is considered to be advantageous, as it's the middle ground between too much suffering in the lower realms and too little suffering in the higher destinations. A human life is a rare opportunity, they say: the perfect blend of pain and pleasure makes us uniquely able to learn the teachings that lead to Awakening, and we should not squander the opportunity.

Buddhism is not alone in embracing the concept of karma. The notion that every action affects future rebirths is a common feature of many Indian religious and philosophical traditions. But Buddhists do differ from most of these other traditions in that they place a lot of importance on the intention behind our actions. As one of my meditation teachers, S. N. Goenka (1924–2013), used to illustrate it: Imagine a person pulls out a blade and slices open someone's abdomen, and that person dies. But in one case the assailant is an assassin trying to kill the victim, and in another case it's a surgeon performing an emergency procedure in an attempt to save their life. While the person's actions and the resulting death are the same in both cases, the karmic effect is very negative in the first case and very positive in the second. The intentions behind the action matter above all else.

Buddhists do not only use karma to talk about how actions affect the conditions of the next life. This theory also has something to say about how our actions affect our present lives. There are a lot of popular Buddhist stories in which the effects of someone's actions rebound immediately. For example, one legend about the Indian Buddhist King Ashoka says that he lost all of his wealth at one point in time, leaving him with nothing but half of a medicinal fruit. But, out of genuine generosity, Ashoka donated that fruit to the sangha, the Buddhist monastic community, in order to make a soup that cured their illnesses. Because of the good karma earned through that single act of generosity, he soon regained all of his former glory and became even more rich and powerful than before.

These kinds of narratives, as well as the jataka tales about the previous lives of the Buddha, are in many ways similar to Aesop's fables, Bible stories, and other folktales in the way they are designed to communicate clear and simple moral messages. Of course, Buddhist philosophers have provided much more fine-grained expositions of the intricacies of how karma works. But most devout Buddhist practitioners don't dwell on the details. It is enough simply to know that acts of generosity, kindness, and care for others can earn us good karma.

In this simplified view, karma works sort of like a bank account: positive karmic merit can be stored up in order to offset negative karma that was accumulated earlier in this life or in previous lives. In most traditions of Buddhism, this karmic merit is also transferrable from one person to another. It is therefore quite common for people performing good deeds to dedicate the merit they earn to another person. You might, for example, dedicate merit to someone who is ill or who has very recently died and who is seen as needing a quick shot of good karma to ensure birth in a fortunate destination. (When someone dies, they are often thought to be stuck for a period of weeks in a limbo state—in English usually known by the Tibetan term *bardo*—during which gifts of karmic merit can make a difference for their future.)

Alternatively, you might dedicate the merit of an action to all sentient beings everywhere. In all cases, because you are donating the merit you have earned rather than hoarding it for yourself, this is considered to be doubly meritorious and earns you even more good karma. However, since the intentions matter more than the actions, if you are engaging in merit-making or merit-transference simply out of greed for merit, then the whole thing is nullified.

This view of karma as something like a cosmic bank account with credits and debits is extremely widespread among Buddhists. In most times and places throughout history, becoming a monk or nun, seriously following the Path, practicing meditation, and following in the Buddha's footsteps toward Awakening was undertaken only by a very small number of people. Most Buddhists have thought these ideals are far too difficult to actually put into practice in this lifetime. It's not at all a stretch to say that the vast majority of Buddhists who have ever lived—including most Buddhists throughout the world today—have taken merit-making as their main practice over and above anything listed in the Eightfold Path.

You might already be able to intuit that the idea of a law of ethics that operates on the basis of intention can lead to confusing situations in which the meritorious thing to do is exceedingly difficult to untangle. Let me give you an example that happened to me one of the first times I visited a Buddhist temple in Thailand. In front of the temple, a woman had set up a stall where she was selling birds in small bamboo cages. The idea was to buy a bird from her and set it free. Since you're liberating a living being from suffering, this is considered an act of generosity that will earn you some merit. That's nice, I thought initially. But as I investigated further, I found that the woman's son was catching the released birds with a net behind the temple. He was putting them back into cages and returning them to his mother in order for her to sell them again and again.

It turns out that this is a very common scenario in Buddhist countries, but the first time I saw it I was quite perplexed. What are the karmic implications here? My first impulse was to buy a bird, to do a good deed by freeing it. But then I discovered that by buying a bird, I was in fact supporting an operation that was repeatedly ensnaring birds, causing them suffering for profit. Knowing that, should I buy a bird or not? Maybe not.

Thinking further, though, I could also see the karmic entanglements of this operation for the woman and her son. They are trapping birds and holding them for ransom. Surely, that must be bad karma for them. But, by doing so, they are giving the temple visitors the opportunity to make merit, which surely must mean good karma for them. So, maybe I should support their operation after all, because it's generating beneficial karma for lots of people?

But wait! As I thought about it even further, I discovered another layer of consideration. As a Western traveler in Thailand, I have a lot more privilege and money than this rural Thai family who has to engage in such a paradoxical profession in order to eke out a living. Maybe, I thought, I should buy the whole lot of birds at once and set them all free. Maybe I should buy the bird-sellers out for the whole day so they can go home. And then, to top it off, I'll dedicate the merit of this action to the mother and son, hoping that they might get lucky and escape their present economic condition.

Ah, yes, but then, won't I have sent the message to the community that you can potentially earn a lot of money from tourists in this bird-trapping profession? And won't then even more people be out here tomorrow trapping and selling birds?

What's the best thing to do in this situation? What would you have done? Well, karma usually won't give you a straight answer about what's right and what's wrong. It's not a black-or-white system of rules or a simple equation. It's more like a framework for thinking through the ethical implications of your decisions within a larger picture that is ever expanding and becoming more complex. It's a self-reflective practice that asks you to take into account an increasing number of variables each time you look at it. The birds in the cage are just one small example of how complex ethics can get once you start thinking with karma. More complicated scenarios, such as politics, war, or climate change, involve many more variables. Sorting out the right thing to do in real-life situations involving countless different actors who are affected in different ways can be enormously difficult. From a Buddhist perspective, the approach would be to try to see all of the options for action in any situation, to understand all of the implications of each, to know all of your own intentions clearly, and then to make the best choice that benefits all sentient beings.

Clearly, what Buddhism is asking of us is exceedingly difficult or even impossible. But while ordinary people may struggle to parse the complexity of such ethical questions, they say that a fully Awakened person attains a perfectly clear-eyed understanding of karma. In fact, in the legend of the Buddha's life, he is said to have seen all the karma from all of his lives on the night he sat under the bodhi tree. Having this realization broke karma's hold over him and liberated him from the cycle of rebirth. As an Awakened person, he no longer could produce karma through his actions, because his intentions were always pure. Thus, when he passed away, the Buddha attained complete and total liberation from rebirth in samsara.

Ordinary people will struggle to see the right course of action until we ourselves are liberated, but meanwhile we can continually strive toward this ideal. Knowing that it is difficult for us to see karma clearly, the Buddha gave some minimum criteria for living an ethical life. His Five Precepts include avoiding killing any sentient beings, taking what's not yours, sexual misconduct, untruthful speech, and intoxication. These are often presented as the mandatory rules for all Buddhists, but don't get any romanticized ideas that all Buddhists actually follow them. Like the Ten Commandments or other religious moral codes, the Five Precepts describe an ideal to strive for rather than the actual lived experience of most people. But the precepts give some basic guidelines that many people have found helpful as a starting point toward living a more ethical and responsible life.

The Five Precepts at first glance seem straightforward enough, but these too can be interpreted as starting points for deeper ethical thinking rather than as ironclad laws. If we think about them using the multistep process I introduced above, they can get complicated very quickly. For example, take the first precept. It's easy enough to avoid intentionally killing sentient beings with your own hands. But what about your consumer choices—buying meat or leather goods, let's say—that cause beings to be killed by others? Okay, you say, so I'll become a vegan. But even if you buy only plant-based foods, aren't you contributing to the death of beings as their habitats are cleared to make room for agricultural fields? If you drive a car, aren't you contributing to climate change that kills off species? Even if you hold perfectly still and do nothing, if you know that there are sentient beings dying that you could help, yet you do nothing to intervene, aren't you contributing to their death through your inaction? Upon deeper investigation, don't most of our decisions as modern human beings result in harm of some sort or another to other beings? How can we possibly navigate this thicket of contradictions and interconnections? Is it even possible to live an ethical life?

Thinking in terms of karma doesn't give us pat answers to these questions, but it gives us tools to help move past a simplistic understanding of ethics. It invites us to question our actions from multiple angles and to evaluate our choices and their consequences in the broadest terms. For me, it's here that the Buddhist notion of karma is most useful. Personally, I am not interested in making the argument that karma is true in a scientific sense—that people are literally reborn. I think the idea of karma is most valuable as an extended metaphor. Even if we do not believe in rebirth, I think karma can still be a useful tool to help us to think more clearly about our decisions in a useful and productive way, in order to gain perspective on how our actions affect the other beings around us.

By the way, after some consideration, I bought three birds that day outside the temple. What would you have done?

5

RENUNCIATION

In the myth of the Buddha's life introduced in the first chapter of this book, Siddhartha displays many virtues. But one of the most dominant values in the story is renunciation. This is the next stop on our tour of the most important Buddhist ideas.

As mentioned in the previous chapter, many Buddhists don't fully commit to achieving Awakening in this lifetime. They may only embrace a small subset of the many practices laid out by the tradition, hoping to get ahead a bit in this life and waiting to complete the Path in future lifetimes. However, a small minority of Buddhists take inspiration from the story of the Buddha and jump into the quest for perfection with both feet.

Following in the Buddha's footsteps requires a great deal of sacrifice, resolve, and hard work. The new direction that Siddhartha sets out for himself was not a comfortable one. His quest required him to go against the wishes of his family and the expectations of his community. It required him to leave home, even going so far as to abandon his wife and young son. It required him to sever ties with his past and to venture out alone into the forest, into the great unknown. While the going was difficult and his future was uncertain,

Siddhartha knew he must set his spiritual goals above his own desires, his own emotional and material well-being, his instincts for safety, and his habits of complacency.

In his own words, Siddhartha said he was going "against the stream." His quest for Awakening necessitated that he detach from his societal obligations. In leaving his duties as the crown prince of his kingdom behind, he was directly challenging the moral order of early Indian society. Obligations to family, village, and kingdom were in India referred to as one's *dharma*, or one's principal duty in life.

After his Awakening, however, the Buddha's teachings would come to be known as *Buddha-Dharma*. That is to say, early Buddhists conceived of his teachings as a new, higher Dharma that superseded the old rules of the ordinary world. The Buddha's new Dharma announced a higher calling and a nobler Path than following the norms and obligations determined by society. Like a lotus flower rising out of a muddy pond, the Buddha's Dharma asks us to renounce our old selves and to blossom into a higher state. It asks us to make heroic sacrifices in pursuit of our goal and to stop at nothing—not family ties, personal loss, starvation, demons, or anything else—to achieve this transformation.

A certain subset of Buddhists throughout history have embraced the Buddha's model of renunciation in their own lives. For generations since the time of the Buddha, devout Buddhists have "gone forth," which is a euphemism for joining the sangha, the Buddhist monastic community. In most cultures, going forth into the sangha involves detaching from your worldly affairs, such as giving up bank accounts, property, and other assets. It involves giving up your identity by shaving off your hair, wearing robes of some kind (the specifics of robe color and design vary by locale and tradition), and receiving a new name. Going forth usually involves taking vows of celibacy, of honesty, of nonviolence, and making other ethical commitments. And it usually involves leaving home and family behind to live in a monastic setting with other monks and nuns dedicated to a similar lifestyle. (There is also such a thing in some cultures as a Buddhist priest who does not fully renounce in this way—and may, perhaps, retain their possessions, marry, and have children.)

In some cultures, people can ordain and disrobe more than once throughout their lives. In such cases, people can experience the sangha lifestyle at some point in their lives without the need to permanently commit. In Thailand, for example, every Buddhist male traditionally spent some time in the sangha for at least the span of a three-month monsoon season before marrying. Going forth gives people the chance to dip a toe into the sangha for a brief time, in order to see if a long-term commitment is right for them.

When I say "people," though, I don't mean all people. This is a good place to bring up the unpleasant fact that there have always been restrictions on who has the opportunity to officially renounce their social role and join the sangha. People who are physically sick, mentally ill, disabled, or transgender have in virtually all Buddhist cultures historically been excluded.

Women have had a mixed experience. On the one hand, there is a famous story about Mahapajapati Gotami, the Buddha's aunt and stepmother, visiting him after his Awakening and requesting to go forth as one of his followers. The Buddha is said to have refused her request three times, but he changed his mind when he was challenged by one of his chief disciples, Ananda. When Ananda asked him whether women can achieve Awakening, the Buddha answered in the affirmative. Then, Ananda retorted, why should they not be allowed to join the sangha? After some consideration, the Buddha recognized he had been too hasty in denying Mahapajapati Gotami's request, and he conceded.

This story is certainly legendary, but it indicates the ancient Indian sangha's willingness to take a radical stance in a historical time and place in which full female participation in religious life was probably inconceivable to most Indians. That fateful decision has allowed women to play high-profile roles in Buddhism in many cultures over the centuries. When I lived in Taiwan, for example, I was struck by the fact that nuns far outnumbered monks within the ranks of every monastery I visited. (One of the earliest writings in the Buddhist tradition—and, in fact, one of the earliest examples of literature by women anywhere in world history—is the *Therigatha*, a collection of sayings by ancient Indian nuns. Definitely check it out!)

While they have at times been influential, it is also true that women have normally been second-class citizens in nearly all Buddhist monastic settings. The story about Mahapajapati Gotami ends with the Buddha, as a precondition for allowing her to join the order, instituting rules that formally place women under male authority. Women are subordinate to men; even a novice monk who ordained on that very day would be able to sit in front of the most senior nun, though she may have been a member of the community for many decades.

In Southeast Asia, the status of women in the sangha was diminished even further about eight hundred years ago, when the lineage of Buddhist nuns died out. From that time onward, only men could legitimately go forth in that part of the world. Women could continue to participate in Buddhist rituals—and, from what I saw when I lived in Thailand, they usually comprise the majority of participants in any given Buddhist service or observance. They also were able to shave their heads and live in Buddhist temples as permanent residents. But for centuries women were denied the ability to go forth and were always considered to be laypeople rather than full-fledged members of the sangha.

After many centuries, change addressing these inequalities began in the 1980s and '90s, when women started to successfully reclaim the right to go forth. An organization called Sakyadhita International Association of Buddhist Women began orchestrating female ordination in Southeast Asia by navigating various technicalities of monastic law. These steps toward equality have been particularly controversial with the conservative Buddhist patriarchy in Thailand, which still frowns upon female members of the sangha. Dhammananda Bhikkhuni, the first Thai woman to go through formal Theravada Buddhist ordination in about eight hundred years, had to travel to Sri

Lanka in order to do so in 2003. Even more strikingly, when Ajahn Brahm, an Australian monk in the Thai Forest sangha lineage, gave ordination to a group of women in 2009, he was excommunicated from the lineage altogether.

But hold on, I can hear you saying, *I thought Buddhism was all about acceptance, tolerance, and peace.* While these kinds of political machinations may seem quite un-Buddhist to the newcomer, I'm not going to present an overly romanticized view of what Buddhism is all about in this book. In fact, once you learn more about it, you'll see that Buddhism is just as fraught with sexism, politics, and infighting as the next religion. It's true that debates and disagreements tend to be legalistic rather than descending quickly into violence, but passions often run high, and injustices certainly are perpetrated in the name of the tradition. (And such conflicts can be violent too, as we'll explore in chapter 17.)

In any event, the whole point of this detour into the politics of ordination here is to underscore how important the matter of renunciation has been for Buddhists, whatever their gender. For many Buddhists, the Path of Buddhism is inseparable from—synonymous with, even—renouncing the world.

When I first encountered Buddhism, the story of the Buddha and its model of renunciation spoke to me strongly. Wanting to experience this lifestyle for myself, I eventually decided to become a resident layperson in a Thai Forest sangha monastery for the rainy season, just to see what it was all about. I left my fiancée for a time, gave up communication with my family, and even shaved my hair and eyebrows, which is the custom in Thai temples. I moved to a remote part of eastern Thailand, where I wore only white clothes, lived in a sweltering, bug-infested hut in the rainforest, and did a lot of difficult manual labor. I also gave up all entertainment, subsisted on one meal per day, and got very little sleep. The lifestyle wasn't easy, but of course, renunciation isn't renunciation if it's easy!

In the end, my determination wasn't as strong as Siddhartha's. I came back to my fiancée at the end of the rainy season. Happily, she took me back, and we're still married today. That summer I learned that going forth wasn't right for me. I had felt the myth of the Buddha calling to me and had seen how this archetypal ideal could inspire confidence and resolve. But I also had learned that I didn't want to detach from the world.

I'm definitely not alone in struggling with the level of commitment to renunciation that the myth of the Buddha asks of us. I think following the Buddhist Path as it's intended is extremely difficult for most modern people. These days, practicing Buddhism often means doing a bit of mindfulness for a few minutes during the otherwise hectic day, reminding ourselves once in a while to be kind to others, and maybe buying a Buddha statue or some prayer beads (*mala*) as a symbol of peacefulness. Calmness, kindness, and peacefulness are all wonderful virtues, and we should fully support even the smallest efforts to cultivate them in our lives. But let's be honest with ourselves: this kind of practice is a far cry from the Buddha's notion of renunciation!

The Buddhist scholar-practitioner Ronald Purser is a vocal critic of this sort of watered-down Buddhism in his book *McMindfulness*. For Purser, like many other serious practitioners, Buddhism is only Buddhism if it involves detachment, renunciation, sacrifice, and transformation. It's only Buddhism if it poses a radical challenge and upends your comfortable status quo. Rather than make you more relaxed and peaceful, it's actually supposed to hurt quite a bit as you go through a profound transition. Purser argues that, rather than renouncing their old selves, transforming their lives, and embarking on the Path to Awakening, people seem mostly interested in reducing stress just enough to continue to function in the dysfunctional modern world at full tilt.

I can see Purser's point. There is no McMindfulness in Siddhartha's story, is there? He doesn't teach himself to do a few minutes of meditation to take the edge off his stress so he can be a more productive prince. He doesn't buy a few trinkets at the store to remind himself to be peaceful and kind to his subjects. Rather, the story says that he feels the need for Awakening as acutely as a lion shot through the heart with a poisoned arrow. This powerful calling ultimately drives him to walk away from the pinnacle of money and power, abandon his family, leave all his possessions, and go off naked and alone into the forest.

In the myth, the Buddha never could have achieved his tremendous world-shaking victory had he stayed at home and practiced a bit of mindfulness. It is only by making a total break, no matter the cost, and not looking back that he is able to discover a brand-new and completely transformed way of being in the world. Of course, that isn't all there is to it, but his commitment to renunciation is the key that opens up the possibility of Awakening.

In the end, I think the tale of the Buddha's renunciation can inspire us when we need to embrace the spirit of letting go of the familiar and the safe in our own lives. But it also challenges us. It asks us: What would you be willing to give up in order to achieve the ultimate transformation? Would you be willing to reject the norms and expectations of your own family, your society, and your culture? Would you give up all your money and possessions, your career, and your future? Would you detach from your family—even your kids—if that's what it took to become Awakened? His story leaves us asking ourselves: What possibilities might the universe hold for me? But, also, at what cost? What would I be willing to sacrifice for true happiness? Would I choose to go all the way?

6

NON-SELF

Buddhism is not only asking us to renounce our lifestyle, our money, our comfort, and our time. All of that would be relatively easy in comparison to its main demand. The goal of the Eightfold Noble Path is, in fact, a much more difficult form of renunciation: renouncing the self. Renouncing the self may sound weird, undesirable, or even dangerous. But according to basic Buddhist theory, our sense of self is the source of a deep delusion (in Sanskrit, *maya*) that haunts us throughout our lives. The sooner we see through it, the better.

This is tricky topic, and if you're not up for a philosophical discussion, feel free to skim through this chapter. But if you're interested in learning about this tradition, since renouncing the self is the central premise of Buddhism, you might have no choice but to dive right in.

I think the best place to start is with a quick word about how "self" is understood in contemporary science, which will help us to put these Buddhist ideas into perspective. Cutting-edge research in the fields of neurology and cognitive science is demonstrating that the sense that each of us is an individual self is the result of a particular sort of brain activity. The continuous, persistent sense of being "me" is a not just a reflection of the way that things are but rather is a feeling that is being generated by my brain at an unconscious level. For the rest of this chapter, we'll put aside the science and take Buddhism's account of the self—or the lack thereof—on its own terms. But I wanted to start off by suggesting that Buddhism's claim that you can destabilize the process of "selfing" and arrive at a state of "non-self" (*anatman*) is not as preposterous an idea as it might initially sound.

According to Buddhist philosophy, at the most basic level, what we call the self is generated by the interconnections between five separate things. In Sanskrit, these are called "heaps" (*skandhas*). First, we have the heap of the physical body. This seems to us as if it is a solid object, the house, so to speak, in which our consciousness lives. However, in ancient India they emphasized that the body is a compounded thing. It was commonly believed that physical objects were constructed out of the Great Elements—tiny particles of earth, water, fire, and wind, which intermingled and combined together in space. The worldview in ancient times was different than our modern knowledge of atoms and subatomic particles, but you can think of the Indian theory as somewhat analogous. What appears to the naked eye to be a solid object is, at the microscopic level, a cluster of bits and pieces coming and going in a constant flurry of change. Ultimately, all physical forms are characterized by their impermanence (*anitya*). Change may happen slowly or instantaneously, but no physical forms stay the same forever.

In the same way that the physical body seems solid but is really made up of a fluctuating heap of particles, the processes of the mind are also made up of heaps of tiny impermanent mental events. In fact, the remaining four heaps that make up the self are all mental. There is a heap made up of our cognition or conscious awareness, a heap of perceptions that come in via our senses (sights, sounds, feelings, and other sensory inputs), a heap of feelings that we experience about our conscious experience (liking, disliking, etc.), and a heap of mental formations (words, images, volitions, desires, memories, and thoughts). These mental heaps flow through our awareness so fast that we don't notice their true nature as separate things. Because we don't discriminate between these processes and don't see their impermanence on a moment-by-moment basis, they all get clumped together. Thoughts and feelings that identify this clump of experiences as "mine" are what produce a sense of self. As selves, we then cling to these mental experiences, wanting to hang on to them, avoid them, or otherwise control them. Not realizing the impermanent and non-self nature of all these five heaps is, according to Buddhism, the fundamental illusion that defines the human experience. This is the primary cause of our duhkha, the source of all of our suffering, unhappiness, and dissatisfaction.

Awakening, as the term is used in Buddhism, is the opposite of all of this. It means fully recognizing that the sense of self is a construct and understanding how this construct is built—not just on an intellectual level but actually being able to perceive the impermanence of the moment-by-moment flow of mental events. It means clearly seeing how the heaps are constantly changing, how this whole process is actually devoid of any inherent selfhood, and how clinging to a notion of "me" produces suffering. Buddhists call this seeing "reality as it is" (*yatha bhuta*).

The problem with trying to see "reality as it is" is that it is difficult to actually perceive any of the heaps clearly in real time. As soon as we attempt to closely investigate any of them, most of us are swiftly carried away by a river of sensations, thoughts, and feelings that is beyond our control. We become distracted: lost in imaginations, memories, anxieties, or daydreams. Our clarity is clouded by a whole host of mental afflictions (*kleshas*): anger, fear, anxiety, lust, greed, jealousy, pride, and all sorts of other destructive emotions and delusions. We find ourselves wrapped up in it all: striving after certain things we want, wishing certain things were different, being dissatisfied with our current situation, or telling ourselves stories and then reacting to them as if they were true.

The mental phenomena we each experience is uniquely our own, and no two people have the same internal landscape. Here is where karma comes into the equation again. Previously, we talked about karma as what determines rebirth, but according to Buddhist theory it also has consequences for our moment-to-moment experience of the world. It makes a difference if we've been filling our lives with negativity, anger, hatred, violence, lying, cheating, stealing, and harming others. All of this will result in more negative mental chatter. Living a more ethical life, on the other hand, results in a moment-to-moment mental experience that is less harsh, less anxious, and less negative. I think we all know this from everyday experience: just think how much anxiety you have and how much more mental work you have to do when keeping track of a lie than if you had just told the truth from the beginning.

Even if you're an upstanding moral person, however, you still have other individual mental patterns that are standing in the way of your perceiving "reality as it is." Habits of negative self-talk, bad memories, and long-ago traumas, perhaps. Or egotistical thoughts about your previous achievements, goals, and self-importance. All of these mental patterns shape, color, or distort how you see reality at every moment. At the subtlest level, getting absorbed in *any* thought at all is a distraction from clearly seeing. Even if it's a perfectly kind and generous thought, it's still just a thought. By allowing yourself to be absorbed or identified with it, you're getting drawn into one of the heaps instead of seeing the impermanent and non-self nature of the moment.

So that we're not getting too abstract, let's bring all of this down to earth with a concrete everyday scenario that many of us have experienced. Not too long ago, I was driving to work, and a big truck suddenly merged into my lane, cutting me off, causing me to slam on my brakes at the last moment to avoid an accident. As it would for just about anyone, this event resulted in a flurry of quite vivid phenomena for me. Initially, there was a heap of visual perceptions of the truck coming at me, followed by, in rapid-fire succession, the realization of what was happening, feelings of surprise and panic as I swerved and slammed on the brakes, and waves of fear and anxiety. All of these passed through my mental awareness rapidly and chaotically and registered in my body as a raised heart rate and tingling sensations all over my skin. These effects continued to pop up in my awareness for some time after the event, and I even felt some of them still buzzing around my mind and body when I got to work and retold the story to a colleague. For some people, the disconcerting effects might have continued to crop up for the rest of the day or even in dreams that night.

All of the perceptions, feelings, and reactions that arose in the midst of the situation are to be expected. Every normal person would at least momentarily be flooded with similar mental phenomena when experiencing such an event. But different people would react differently to these mental phenomena. Someone whose karma (i.e., their previous actions, intentions, and experiences) has predisposed them in one particular direction might primarily experience feelings of anger. This person might get carried away, aggressively honk their horn, and maybe even follow the truck to the next traffic light, jump out of their car, and perpetrate a violent act inspired by road rage. Someone else experiencing the same event, because of their own unique karma, might identify more strongly with fear. Getting lost in that feeling, they might experience cascades of anxiety or panic for days and weeks to come.

As for me, fortunately, I had a less severe reaction than these two hypothetical people, recovering my poise more quickly and moving on with my life. But regardless of the intensity of the reaction, anyone who experienced this situation would have a feeling that something had happened to "me" on the way to work. They would identify all the physical and mental phenomena as belonging to "me," as part of "me," or as part of "my" experience.

A similar process is being repeated again and again through countless less-dramatic situations that happen all day long throughout our lives. Let's say it's a conversation with your partner, during which you feel certain emotions and react in certain ways to your partner's words or tone. Or an email arrives that triggers emotions and reactions just based on your first glance of the subject line. Or you experience pleasant mental phenomena when you step outside into the warm spring air or taste a great meal or greet your dog upon returning home at the end of the day. In all of these cases, these experiences are streams of sensations, perceptions, thoughts, and emotions running through our minds and bodies. In all cases, we may become absorbed in certain aspects of our own mental phenomena in individually unique ways due to our karma (both the patterns of our entire lives as well as the specific conditions at that very moment). In all cases, certain thoughts may come up, or certain memories may be triggered in response to these stimuli. These thoughts and memories would then produce more sensations, feelings, and other mental phenomena that we would react to.

In all of these situations, we inevitably feel a sense of ownership over the sensations, feelings, perceptions, thoughts, and emotions that pass through our awareness. We perceive our experiences as belonging to us. But Buddhism raises the question whether there actually is a self sitting there amidst all of those heaps of impermanent phenomena. Take a moment to reflect on it: If there is a self in there, where would it be? I think we can agree that the self can't be a momentary visual perception, a feeling of surprise or anger, a reaction to a physical stimulus, or a memory. The self can't be a single fleeting moment of frustration or anxiety or pleasure or love. Nor can the self be defined as the physical body, this heap of material particles.

Most of us have a sense that the self is some kind of entity that is stable at the center of our experiences, one that is experiencing all of the phenomena taking place. But ponder this question for yourself: Where exactly is that witness located? Can you say? Have you ever looked for it? Have you ever found it? This very question—"Where is the self?"—is the starting point of the Buddhist exploration of "reality as it is."

As is true of some of the other concepts we explored earlier, questioning the existence of the self is not unique to Buddhism. It is a common issue in all kinds of religion and philosophy, and is a specific focal point for Indian traditions in particular. Many other traditions have concluded that the self is an awareness, a consciousness, a soul, God, or some other entity that encompasses or transcends or witnesses all of the phenomena we experience. Buddhism differs from these by concluding that there is no self at all. Buddhism says that if you actually look for this self, you will find thoughts about being a self, a feeling that you are you, or a sense that you are witnessing your life happening, but you will never find a self that exists as a separate entity apart from the five heaps. Buddhism says that if you get better and better at concentrating on your constantly changing mental experience, you'll find at the bottom of it all not a permanent self, but only a constant stream of impermanent, ever-changing phenomena.

There's a lot more to these ideas that we won't be able to touch on in this brief chapter, but I will add that the goal of most forms of Buddhist meditation is realizing the illusory nature of the sense of self and seeing clearly the impermanence at the bottom of human existence. The culmination of the Eightfold Path is using meditation practice to unbind us from our identification with the five heaps and learning to abide in the impermanence that is left once the sense of a stable self is deconstructed. This process, the texts warn us, is not comfortable. It can feel quite threatening, destabilizing, and out of control. It can lead people into uncertain territory and occasionally produce unwelcome side-effects. However, when, finally, after much practice, all things without exception can be clearly seen as impermanent and devoid of self, the illusion finally loses its grip.

Deconstructing the self in this way might sound pessimistic or nihilistic, but, for Buddhists, seeing "reality as it is" evokes a sense of tremendous freedom. Arriving at this realization, we are liberated from identifying with the chaotic, raging flow of mental and physical phenomena. We see the dissatisfaction and suffering we have been producing by taking all of these impermanent heaps so personally. We can be truly at peace with the constant fluctuations of events, thoughts, and emotions, not attached to trying to control or identify with them. We have finally vanquished all suffering.

Buddhists constantly emphasize that using words to explain the ultimate truth is impossible. Be that as it may, impermanence and non-self have attracted thousands of years of philosophical speculation and intellectual elaboration, and mountains of literature have been written attempting to describe them. Of course, as with all other aspects of Buddhism, different schools of thought and different cultural traditions have proposed different (sometimes completely divergent) ways of speaking about this. Different Buddhist traditions also have different views about the process of Awakening, and we'll explore those in the coming chapters. That being said, there is a nearly universal way of speaking among Buddhists about overcoming the tyranny of the self: it is complete and utter freedom.

Can you sense this freedom from my description above? Maybe give it a try next time you get cut off in traffic or in some other situation in which you feel intensely negative. Don't try to control your reactions; just observe what's happening "as it is." Do the negative feelings flow through more easily? Do you feel lighter than you normally would? Don't take my word for it, but notice for yourself. Only you can say whether or not this perspective helps you.

7

BUDDHA

It is now time to turn to one of Buddhism's most important ideas, which so far we have gotten away without addressing: what exactly is a Buddha? We met Siddhartha Gautama in the very first chapter, and I have described a number of concepts to help describe what makes him different from ordinary people. So far, we know that a Buddha is a person recognized as an Awakened One. We know that Awakening is equivalent to attaining human perfection, and that it comes at the end of a long path of practice and many lifetimes of good karma. We also know that the core characteristic of Awakening is the liberation from suffering that comes from giving up all identification with the self.

Our picture, thus far, is an accurate one for nearly all forms of Buddhism. But in order to answer the question of what a Buddha is in more detail, we will need to introduce the five major categories of Buddhism that exist in the world today, because each one answers this question differently. Each one of these schools claims to be the original or the most authentic type. However, from a strictly historical perspective, whatever form of Buddhism originally existed in ancient India disappeared long ago. Each of the currently existing traditions emerged in distinct times and places many centuries after the supposed lifetime of Siddhartha Gautama, many thousands of miles away from the origin point of Buddhism in northeastern India. Since their emergence, each has undergone many changes throughout history, shaping each of these traditions in radically different ways. Each subsequently developed radically different ideas of what it means to be a Buddha.

In my opinion, these traditions are so different from one another that we'd probably be better off if we considered them different religions. However, they generally are referred to as schools or traditions of a single religion called Buddhism. Since we're stuck with that terminology, that's what I'll use in this book as well. A quick warning before we start: As I introduce the five major traditions, I will give a bit of historical and cultural information about each. This chapter therefore will introduce lots of new terminology and information, so it will get a bit more complicated than the previous chapters. It's not important that you memorize the specific details. Above all, note how dramatically different these viewpoints on Buddhahood are from one another. The last three paragraphs of the chapter are especially important, so I would recommend reading them before moving on.

1. THERAVADA

Theravada is a Buddhist tradition with roots in first century BCE Sri Lanka. Historically this school has been most prevalent in Southeast Asia. Today, it is the dominant religion in Sri Lanka, Myanmar, Thailand, Laos, and Cambodia, although like all forms of Buddhism, it is practiced all around the world. This form of Buddhism self-describes as a conservative tradition. Its very name means Teachings of the Elders, indicating that it prioritizes preserving the ways of past generations. This conservatism has certain drawbacks as well as benefits. For example, its reluctance to bend precedent has made it difficult for women to regain the right to ordain as nuns in Theravada countries (see discussion in chapter 5). On the other hand, due to the same reluctance to change, it is also true that some Theravada practices are done the same way they were centuries ago, and this historic preservation of tradition is a point of great pride for practitioners of this school. In Theravada Buddhism, the Awakening of a Buddha is considered an epochal event. There can only be one Buddha in any given aeon (often measured as five thousand years), and Siddhartha Gautama was it. A Buddha, by this definition, is a special sort of man (yes, they are always male!) born into the world at a time when the Dharma is unknown, and he works out his own Path to rediscover it. Once Awakened, he then teaches this Path, so that those who follow his teachings can become Awakened themselves. The people who become Awakened by following him are not technically buddhas but rather are referred to as *arhat*, or "worthies." When worthies eventually die, they are said to be released into a final Nirvana, liberated from the cycle of rebirth and permanently extinguished.

In fact, the Sanskrit word Nirvana literally translates as "blowing out." This is probably the single most misunderstood concept in the whole Buddhist repertoire. In everyday English, we usually use Nirvana to mean "bliss" or "joy," and lots of people assume that Buddhist meditation is all about experiencing happiness, when it really means the complete cessation of all experience.

2. MAHAYANA

The second major tradition of Buddhism calls itself *Mahayana*, the Great Vehicle. This school historically emerged in the first centuries CE in northwestern India. It rapidly spread via the Silk Roads and became the most widespread form of Buddhism in the ancient world. At one point, its influence stretched across a huge territory from eastern Iran to Japan and from Mongolia to Indonesia. Today, Mahayana is the predominant form of Buddhism in East Asia (i.e., China, Korea, Japan, and Vietnam). In contrast to the conservatism of Theravada, this tradition characterizes itself as a more inclusive, more flexible, more universal form of Buddhism than what came before. In fact, because it's so diverse internally, it's most helpful to think of Mahayana not as a single tradition of Buddhism but as a whole branch of the Buddhist family tree.

We will talk more about some of Mahayana's central ideas in future chapters, but for now, let's focus on its notion of Buddhahood. There are divergent opinions among different Mahayana groups, but altogether they present a radical departure from earlier Buddhism. Many types of Mahayana say that there are countless alternative worlds or dimensions throughout the universe that each have their own buddhas simultaneously. Not only are there multiple worlds with different buddhas, but each of those buddhas in turn has three different types of bodies. They have an eternal "Dharma body" (*dharmakaya*), which is synonymous with the very nature of Buddhahood itself. They also have innumerable "enjoyment bodies" (*sambhogakaya*) made out of bliss or out of light, which can be manifested in meditation, in visions, or in paradises called Pure Lands. They also can generate "manifestation bodies" (*nirmanakaya*), bodies that take on material form in order to be born, to live, and to die in the ordinary physical world.

According to this interpretation, Siddhartha Gautama (who is usually referred to by Mahayanists by the name Sakyamuni) was physically born into our world in a particular time and place in order to serve as our Buddha. However, this was actually just one of the many manifestation bodies of the Great Sun Buddha, Vairocana, who is constantly manifesting bodies of various types. Because buddhas have complete power over their manifestation bodies, Mahayana scriptures often present Sakyamuni engaging in various displays of miraculous powers: he can fly, grow huge, emit light, or even unfurl his tongue to reach all the way up to the heavens.

A Mahayana text called the *Nirvana Sutra* depicts the death of Sakyamuni. While on his deathbed, he lets his close disciples know that he's not really dying. He reveals that his whole life has all just been a mirage, a big show put on to teach his followers about the Noble Path of non-self and liberation from duhkha. One of his manifestation bodies may be passing away from this physical world, but his indestructible Dharma body lives on eternally.

In addition to Sakyamuni, Mahayana practitioners also pray, chant, and perform rituals seeking the assistance of other buddhas from other worlds. The most popular of these alternative buddhas is Amitabha, Infinite Light, who has a Pure Land far to the west of here. Amitabha is particularly revered by Mahayana practitioners because he promised that anyone who recites his name could be reborn in this paradisiacal realm, where the trees are made out of jewels and all your wishes come true. Another Mahayana Buddha is Bhaisajyaguru, the Master of Medicines, whose Pure Land is far to the east. Practitioners revere this Buddha when the going gets tough, because he promised to help eradicate diseases, premature death, and other karmic calamities for those who call upon him.

Do you know who is not one of the Mahayana buddhas? That fat, jolly Chinese guy with the long floppy earlobes that pretty much everyone in the West mistakenly calls the Buddha. It's understandably confusing, because his name in Chinese is pronounced "Budai," which is not the Chinese word for "Buddha" but literally means "cloth sack." Budai was an eccentric Buddhist monk from the tenth century who, over time, became a common symbol of happiness, luck, and prosperity. People say that he is a bodhisattva (see chapter 12) who is destined to become a Buddha in the future. But he's not a Buddha yet. I like to think of Budai as a Chinese Santa Claus figure. Next time you see his jolly face, take a closer look. You'll see that he is always surrounded by money, young children, and other signs of happiness, wealth, and family—none of which are symbols of renunciation or non-self.

3. ZEN & 4. VAJRAYANA

As you can already see from the brief description above, Mahayana presents a completely different cosmology—and a completely different view of Buddhahood—from Theravada. On the surface, we can say that buddhas in most forms of Mahayana look a lot more like gods. However, there is yet another understanding of Buddhahood that also is quite central to some particular schools of Mahayana that is again different from other traditions. This viewpoint is particularly important in the third and fourth Buddhist traditions I will introduce: Zen and Vajrayana.

We'll talk in more detail about Zen in future chapters (particularly chapter 16). For now, I can say that it is a form of Mahayana that emerged in China in the sixth and seventh centuries CE, although it really took off in the tenth to thirteenth centuries. Zen was heavily influenced by the native East Asian tradition of Daoism, and it spread from China to Korea, Japan, and Vietnam. In English this tradition is usually called Zen, which is the Japanese pronunciation of the Chinese word *chan*, which in turn is a Chinese pronunciation of the Sanskrit word *dhyana*, which simply means "meditation." So one could say that Zen is calling itself the meditation school of Buddhism. Its most influential leaders have normally emphasized a commitment to meditation instead of prayers and other types of devotions. By refocusing on serious meditation, Zen was in many ways reacting against the complex and imaginative Mahayana pantheon I just described.

Right around the same time Zen was first taking shape in China, another Mahayana tradition called *Vajrayana* was emerging in northern India. This form of Buddhism developed at the height of the Tantric movement, and it shares many features with the Tantric forms of Hinduism that also developed at this time. It spread to Tibet before disappearing from India around 1200 CE. While it is most widely known in the West in its Tibetan form, Vajrayana also was historically influential in Mongolia, Nepal, Bhutan, parts of western China and Russia, and as far away as Cambodia and Indonesia. It has also long coexisted alongside Zen and other forms of Mahayana in Japan, where it is commonly referred to as Esoteric Buddhism.

The name Vajrayana means the Vajra Vehicle, referring to a magic-wandlike scepter that plays a role in certain rituals in this tradition (the word also means a diamond or a thunderbolt). One basic idea of all Tantric religions is that, while ordinary forms of religious practice are good for the general public, there are more advanced techniques available for those who are "in the know." Vajrayana thus offers initiation into secret lineages, in which practitioners study closely guarded techniques under the supervision of a guru, or Awakened teacher. These practices are said to be powerfully transformative, like a magic vajra, able to zap people into full Awakening instantaneously.

Although both Zen and Vajrayana are forms of Mahayana, these traditions are typically characterized by a very different notion of Buddhahood than was introduced in the previous section. The basic idea in both schools is that you actually *are* a Buddha already. That is to say, every person already has within them a Buddha-nature or an essential nature that is already Awakened. You may not currently realize it, because your true nature as a Buddha is obscured from your view, but Awakening is there right under your nose even now. Nothing you ever do can shatter or mar its luminous perfection. The task in these forms of Buddhism, then, is not to achieve Buddhahood but to learn to manifest the Buddhahood that is already there. We'll come back to this topic in chapter 9 to try to make some sense of it. For the moment, we need to move on to introduce one last alternative notion of Buddhahood.

5. BUDDHIST MODERNISM

In addition to the four traditional forms of Buddhism I've described so far, there is one last major category of Buddhism that most scholars (and some practitioners) call Buddhist modernism. This term refers to many disparate nontraditional Buddhist groups that have emerged in the last hundred years or so, as well as to modern reinterpretations or reconfigurations of the traditional forms of Buddhism discussed above. Across all of these different groups and sects, Buddhist modernists have a radically different view of Buddhahood than those that have been introduced thus far, one notably more in synch with modern science and secularism.

Buddhist modernism arose in the 1800s. At that time, Buddhism all across Asia—whether in Theravada, Mahayana, Zen, or Vajrayana contexts—started going through major transformations. European colonialists, Christian missionaries, and international public opinion criticized Buddhism as superstitious and backward. In response, both Asian Buddhists and Western scholars embarked on a process of rein-terpreting, reforming, and modernizing Buddhism to better conform to modern sensibilities. They rejected what they saw as unnecessary "cultural baggage" and sought to restore what they saw as the "true es-sence" of Buddhism. That process picked up steam in the 1900s and is still ongoing today. Buddhist modernism is the result of these efforts.

For most Buddhist modernists, Siddhartha Gautama is neither a special person born with an epochal destiny nor a manifestation of a cosmic god. He is instead often characterized as a man who was an ancient scientist or psychologist who discovered the inner workings of the human mind through empirical investigation. Many modern Buddhists would also insist that his teachings are fully secular and fully scientific. Rejecting the notion that Buddhism has anything to do with divine beings or supernatural powers, they argue that—un-derneath the optional cultural symbolism and customs—it is simply an objective and naturalistic description of "reality as it is."

The reinterpretation of Buddhism in order to make it compatible with a modern worldview—or at the very least, to establish a mod-ern vocabulary for talking about Buddhist ideas—has been wildly successful around the world. In English-speaking countries, you can find variations of Buddhist modernism under names such as Secular Buddhism and the Mindfulness Movement. Each of these groups now has a growing number of related books, websites, podcasts, and other materials. Their proponents are notable in how they reframe Bud-dhism as secular rather than religious and draw heavily on scientific evidence.

Given the stark differences between these five views of Buddhahood, you can see why it would be easy to get confused by contradictory messages if you didn't know any better. Whenever you pick up a book about Buddhism, it is critical to know what school the author comes from if you are going to understand what they are saying. In this chapter, I've included some keywords and some cultural and historical context for each of the five types of Buddhism in order to help you determine which type you are reading about in the future. At the very least, you'll want to keep separate in your mind the terms Theravada, Mahayana, Zen, Vajrayana/Esoteric/Tibetan Buddhism, and Buddhist modernism.

If it all seems like a blur at the moment, I promise that as you get more familiar with the five different traditions, you will naturally get better and better at appreciating their differences. To use a rather non-Buddhist metaphor: it's kind of like drinking wine. Didn't they all taste the same to you at first, and didn't you keep getting confused about which was which? The more you learned, though, the better you could discriminate between them. First you learned to taste the difference between red and white, and then you learned to separate Pinot Noir from Merlot and Cabernet. Over time, you may have continued to refine your knowledge until you could taste the difference between French, Californian, and Chilean versions of the same grape or even start to identify specific vintages.

If you're not into wine, translate that analogy to craft beer, coffee, music, or whatever else it is that you personally like to geek out about. I don't know an awful lot about wine myself, but I am a certifiable geek on the topic of Buddhism. I'll admit that when I see people mishmashing Buddhist traditions together without trying to understand their differences, I do kind of feel as a wine lover might when watching someone indiscriminately dump a bunch of different wines together into the same vat and then chug down the result without really tasting it. Of course, there are some blended wines that taste pretty good. But I'm hoping that this chapter has helped you start noticing and appreciating the differences between different vintages of Buddhism—and learning to enjoy their diversity and flavor for their own sake.

8

MINDFULNESS

Have you noticed the craze about mindfulness that's really been picking up steam over the last ten years? Maybe that's what piqued your interest in Buddhism in the first place? In this chapter we will focus on mindfulness, the most influential form of meditation across the spectrum of Buddhist traditions.

Much of the popularity of mindfulness meditation in the West is due to the work of Dr. Jon Kabat-Zinn (b. 1944), professor emeritus of medicine at the University of Massachusetts. Kabat-Zinn started a lab in 1979 to investigate the stress-reducing applications of Buddhist meditation. Since that time, mindfulness-based stress reduction (MBSR) has become almost synonymous with Buddhism for many people in the modern world. But mindfulness, although it tends to get a lot of the limelight, is really just one part of the overall Buddhist approach to meditation.

In English, we use the word "meditation" to translate a variety of different words from various languages—including *jhana, bhavana, dhyana, chan, zen,* and *gom*—that have different shades of meaning within different Buddhist schools and cultural traditions. The previous chapter introduced five major forms of Buddhism and discussed the radically different views on Buddhahood espoused by each. With such disagreement over what Buddhahood means, there are a predictably large number of contradictory ideas about how we should practice in order to make progress on the Path toward Buddhahood. However, it is true that most forms of Buddhism advocate some kind of contemplative technique as the core training leading to Awakening.

Some Buddhist meditations are intended to improve the quality of the thoughts and reflections flowing through your stream of consciousness. (We will cover some of these practices in chapter 13.) Others are about reconnecting with your body and optimizing your health and wellness. (We'll discuss these in chapter 15.) Some meditations include chanting a *mantra* or mentally repeating a particular word. Other forms direct practitioners to concentrate on a visual image, such as a picture of a Buddha or another special person, or a symbol, shape, or color. Mindfulness, however, is a form of meditation that is directed toward understanding the mind, deconstructing the sense of self, and seeing "reality as it is."

When Buddhists talk about mindfulness, they are normally referring to the practice of focusing your attention on a particular object and trying to remember to pay attention to it. In fact, the word "mindfulness" is a translation of the Buddhist term *sati* or *smriti*, which literally means "to remember," "to recollect," or "to bear something in mind." While the object of your mindfulness can be one of a number of different things, the most common Buddhist meditation of all is mindfulness of the breath. Always present, available, and free, the breath is in many ways an ideal meditation object. You breathe tens of thousands of time per day, and although you almost never pay any attention to it, you can learn to.

Getting started is quite easy. If you've never done any meditation before, try this now: For the next two or three minutes, try to be aware of each breath you take. Set a timer so you don't have to watch the clock, and then put your attention onto your breath. See if you can capture each inhalation and exhalation, without missing any. Most people place their attention either on their nose, so they can feel the breath coming in and out of the nostrils, or somewhere in the abdomen, so they can feel the rise and fall of the diaphragm. Some people mentally count each breath to see how many they can notice before they get distracted. Usually you don't change the breath in any way; just watch it going in and out as it normally does.

Did you try it for a few minutes? If so, you probably found that you could pay attention to a few breaths at a time—maybe even a few dozen—but then you got distracted by some thought or emotion or physical sensation. Your mind probably wandered off for at least a few seconds before you remembered to bring it back to the breath. (Perhaps you wandered off and never came back!) This is the meaning of mindfulness—of *sati*: remembering or recalling. It's the act of again and again remembering to bring your attention back to the breath after it wandered away.

While the breath is most common, another popular object of meditation among Buddhists is body sensations. You can try this one as well. Take a moment right now to see if you can clearly feel a body sensation on your right foot—or any other part of your body. Depending on whether you're sitting, lying down, or standing as you read this, the most obvious place to look might be on the sole of your foot or maybe your heel. But somewhere (anywhere) on your right foot, you should be able to sense a feeling of pressure as it touches your shoe or the floor. Maybe you feel some heat or cold or a tingly sensation? Don't react to the sensation or try to figure it out; just feel it.

Once you can feel a sensation on one part of your body, move your attention somewhere else—maybe your other foot; or your back, if you are lying down; or the back of one of your thighs, if you are sitting—and see if you can feel something in the new spot. Now move up to one of your hands, and feel the sensation of this book touching your skin. Do the other. Move to your mouth and feel your tongue and your lips. Like this, continue on through the rest of your body and feel everything bit by bit. Turns out, most people have a body sensation on every square inch of their skin, and you can train yourself to be mindful of that fact just as you can become mindful of the process of breathing.

Once you've played around with body sensations, which really is just the sense of touch, then take a look at your other senses. Hearing, for example. Bring your attention to your ears and hear what sounds there are in the immediate environment. Maybe you've been ignoring them because you're concentrating on reading, but now that you focus on sound, what noises do you hear? Birds, dogs, or cars outside? The faint hum of the air conditioning, a fan, or the fridge? A quiet ringing in your ears? There is probably more than one noise, and some are most likely closer, some farther away. Again, don't react to the noises or try to figure them out; just listen. How long can you pay attention to the sounds flowing into your ears before you get distracted? How many times can you remember to bring your attention back to them?

Once you've given the breath, body sensations, and sounds a try for a few minutes each, you can move to a more advanced practice: mindfulness of thoughts. In the same way that you could choose to perceive the rise and fall of your breath, the sensations in your body, or the sounds coming into your ears, you can also choose to be directly aware of the thoughts passing through your mind. Of all the meditation objects I've mentioned, mindfulness of thoughts is the hardest, because it's difficult not to get involved in your own thoughts. Try it now. Like the other stimuli, don't react to your thoughts or try to figure them out. Just let the river flow by, not identifying with or getting swept up by anything that's coming downstream. Watch in a detached way: there goes a stressful thought about what you've got to do at work tomorrow floating by; there goes a concern about a child; next, a stray reflection about what you ate for dinner; now a pleasant memory from earlier in the week.

Have patience if it feels difficult at first. Whichever of these meditation objects you choose—and some people opt to practice what they call "open awareness" or "open monitoring," meaning they are watching the flow of all of these elements in the present moment simultaneously—you will get better with time. A lot of people start meditating with the expectation that they will immediately become more peaceful or centered. It does happen that some people experience very calm or blissful states early on in their practice of meditation—maybe even during their very first experience—but it's unlikely. That certainly did not happen for me. To be honest, I would say that I've personally had a lot more frustration than bliss during my own experiences with mindfulness meditation. However, over time and with regular practice, I did notice positive changes. No overnight miracles, mind you, but slow and steady improvements.

One crucial thing I've learned during my experience of meditation is that the attention span is trainable. When I started, I could barely pay attention to even three breaths in a row, but over time I learned to stretch the length of time I could remain mindful. In fact, modern scientific studies have found that people can improve their attention span even by practicing just a few minutes per day. In that way, mindfulness is very much like any other mental or physical skill that our brains can learn. If you want to learn how to play tennis or the flute, or to speak Japanese, isn't your best strategy to practice a bit each day and be patient? Maybe you'll never be Serena Williams, but with regular practice, over time, you'll start to see improvement little by little. Maybe sometimes you'll feel like you're plateauing, and sometimes you'll feel like you're backsliding, but if you keep at it, you'll eventually be much better than you are today.

But why, you ask, would anyone want to get good at mindfulness? Tennis is one thing, but of all the skills to learn, why put any time and effort into this one? Well, in my experience, if you consistently practice mindfulness, you will not only get better at paying attention, but you will also gain valuable knowledge about how your mind works. If you're like me, when you first start trying to be mindful of your breath or any other object, you'll see for yourself that your mind is full of mental chatter that is out of control. You'll find that no matter how hard you try to concentrate, you keep getting swept away by the current of mental phenomena. You may also start to see clearly how so much of what's running through your mind is sheer nonsense. You may start to recognize unhelpful or unhealthy patterns of thought.

You may start to understand how you are identifying with your mental phenomena, taking it all personally and even basing your identity on it. You may start to gain some perspective on certain things you thought were so serious or so hard to deal with. In the Buddhist lingo, you may start to train your "monkey mind" instead of letting it rule you.

Some stress reduction programs don't ask for more than ten to twenty minutes a day of mindfulness. However, serious Buddhist meditation traditions may recommend an hour or more of daily practice, as well as periodic retreats where you might sit for ten to twelve hours a day. This level of dedication is considered essential in order to start generating very steady concentration (*samadhi*) and insight (*vipassana*). While such programs normally work with the same meditation objects I've described in this chapter, they usually provide more detailed, intense, and systematic direction.

Buddhist trainings that emphasize concentration often focus on generating what in the Pali language is called *jhana*, advanced states of absorption in which you become so concentrated on the object of meditation that the rest of the world melts away. When everything else disappears, you're left with states of deep bliss, rapture, or stillness. Trainings emphasizing insight, on the other hand, focus on perceiving your chosen object of meditation as a manifestation of suffering, impermanence, and non-self—which in Buddhism are called the "three marks of all existence." This kind of work is more deconstructive, breaking down your mental and physical experience into increasingly finer phenomena. Many training systems call for you to practice both concentration and insight sequentially or simultaneously. Normally, the goal of all of these kinds of advanced practice is to experience "cessations," moments during which the whole self and the world drop away. In other words, Nirvana.

Serious meditation training takes an enormous amount of effort, and there are many ups and downs along the way. My own first experience of meditation was a ten-day silent vipassana meditation retreat outside Bangkok. I was twenty-three at the time, and it was the most impactful event in my life up to that point. I was so struck by my experiences that, afterward, I immediately signed up for two more ten-day sessions in a row. I then went on to attend dozens more similar retreats in Thailand, India, and the United States over the next five years. I became somewhat obsessed with meditation, fixated on experiencing higher states of consciousness.

Eventually, though, I burned out on this kind of practice, and my path took me in a different direction, which I'll talk more about in chapter 13. However, I still highly value all the time I spent on the cushion back in those days. During that first retreat, I came to see myself and my own thought processes clearly for the first time. I began to understand how wrapped up in my emotions and reactions I really was and how all of my priorities were upside down. I also began to see why things were this way, how everything in my life up to that point had shaped who I was. Seeing things so clearly for the first time, I was able to make a permanent transformation in my life. I left behind an impulsive, angry, self-centered childhood and adolescence, and emerged into a new life that was focused on introspection and self-discovery. (Not that there wouldn't be a whole lot more stuff to work through in coming years, mind you!)

Anyway, enough about me. Let's finish up by coming back to the work of Jon Kabat-Zinn that we began the chapter with. There are many other high-profile teachers of Buddhist-style meditation that have been instrumental in popularizing mindfulness training, including revered figures like S. N. Goenka, Thich Nhat Hanh, Jack Kornfield, and Tara Brach. But, more than any other person, it is Kabat-Zinn who has been responsible for bringing mindfulness out of the temple and into the laboratory—and, from there, to hospitals, schools, corporations, and living rooms across the modern world. Building on the mindfulness-training system that Kabat-Zinn began developing in the 1970s, there have been literally thousands of scientific and medical studies conducted on the benefits of mindfulness. This field is still developing, but it is starting to produce interesting results that are worth following. (I've recommended a few of my favorite books on meditation in the resources at the end of the book, including one by Goleman and Davidson, two leading scientists in this research field.)

Buddhists seem split in their opinions about this scientific research. Some are appreciative of the attention that mindfulness is getting, and they applaud the positive PR it provides for Buddhism. Others feel that the meditation protocols used by researchers represent watered-down practices that, in focusing on stress reduction, miss the whole point of Awakening. We don't have to enter this debate here. The upshot is that there are now many different types of workshops, books, and teachings on mindfulness to choose from. Some forms of mindfulness are taught in temples and are fully embedded in specific sectarian Buddhist contexts. Some are taught in lay meditation centers that are more nonsectarian or nontraditional, although there are still some visible Buddhist elements. Still others are taught in psychologists' offices, medical centers, and other secular spaces, and are completely devoid of any Buddhist content. Books on mindfulness can also be similarly categorized on a spectrum from religious to spiritual to medical, and everything in between.

All of this means that, if you decide to take the plunge into meditation practice, there's something out there for everyone. You could, as the Buddhists say, start "practicing as if your hair was on fire" by joining a long-term silent retreat, like I did. Or you could spend a week of ten to fifteen minutes per day focusing, as the podcaster Dan Harris, cofounder of 10% Happier, says, on the more modest aim of becoming just "ten percent happier." You could seek out weekend workshops at your local Buddhist temple, weekly meditation classes at your gym, or use one of the smart phone apps designed to help you establish a daily practice. Whatever method resonates with you is fine. As the Buddhist scriptures famously put it, this teaching is "beneficial in the beginning, beneficial in the middle, and beneficial in the end."

9

BUDDHA-NATURE

Buddha-nature is an idea that comes from the Zen and Tibetan traditions, and like virtually everything else in Mahayana Buddhism, there is a wide range of different interpretations and opinions about it. The core meaning, as I mentioned in chapter 7, is that Awakening is not something to find or work toward; it is already here, innate within you and me and all sentient beings.

The notion that we all have a Buddha-nature does not mean that there is a tiny speck of the Buddha floating around inside our minds or bodies. Rather, it is that underneath, behind, or within all of the ordinary activity of our minds, Awakeness is always already present. Whereas most forms of Buddhism are designed to lead you to Awakening along an arduous Path of mental purification, according to Mahayana Buddhists who embrace the concept of Buddha-nature, we just need to turn our attention around and see what has been going on right under our noses all along.

You can clearly appreciate the difference between these two perspectives by comparing two poems from the *Platform Sutra* (*Tanjing*). The myth behind these poems is that Hongren (601–674), the Fifth Patriarch of Chinese Zen, was looking for a successor, so he hosted a poetry competition to determine who had enough wisdom to deserve this position. One of his most senior disciples wrote a poem succinctly conveying the message of Path-based Buddhism, saying that we need to meditate diligently in order to gradually purify the mind:

> The body is the bodhi tree,
> The mind is like a bright mirror's surface.
> Again and again we diligently wipe it clean,
> So as to prevent any dust.

However, a second poem was dictated in response to the first by an illiterate kitchen assistant named Huineng (638–713) that flipped this idea of making progress toward the goal on its head. Rather than offering an additional admonishment to practice purification, Huineng's verse expressed clearly the insight that one's Buddha-nature is already Awake. Although there are multiple versions, the earliest edition of the *Platform Sutra* relates Huineng's stanza thus:

> Enlightenment has no tree,
> The bright mirror likewise has no surface.
> Buddha-nature is always pristine,
> Where could it be marred by dust?

Guess who was recognized as the Sixth Patriarch?

As you might imagine, modes of practice that assume you are already Awake and just don't realize it are somewhat different from those discussed in the previous chapter on mindfulness. Here, I'll mention three examples of Buddha-nature practices from Japan and Tibet that you may readily encounter in English-language books and workshops. The first is a group of what could be called "formless meditations." These go by different names in different traditions, but some of the main key words include *shikantaza* (which means "just sitting" in Japanese), *dzogchen* ("great perfection" in Tibetan), and *mahamudra* ("great seal" or "great imprint" in Sanskrit). While the specific instructions vary, these meditations are similar in that they do not take any particular thing as a meditation object. Rather, you remain aware of awareness itself. In shikantaza, for example, any time your mind tries to latch onto a specific thing—to think about something, to plan something, to pay attention to something, even to meditate on something—you relax that sense of trying to do something and rest back in formless or contentless awareness.

The second category of practice I'll mention is the Tibetan tradition of "pointing-out instructions." This term usually refers to an interchange or dialogue a practitioner has with a teacher, who uses an exercise or a verbal instruction to turn the practitioner's attention around to see their own already-Awake nature. In Tibetan Buddhism, both pointing-out instructions and formless meditation are considered quite advanced practices, and are taught only after a whole range of preliminary requirements and vows of secrecy. Although Awakeness is already present in everyone from the beginning, there is a concern that these teachings can easily be misunderstood or misconstrued unless one has spent a significant amount of time and energy preparing for the revelation.

The third type of practice is the Zen tradition of *koan* practice. Koans are brief stories or riddles that are intended to shake the practitioner out of their habitual reliance on rational thought. Typically, a koan is assigned to a student who ruminates on the question for a while and reports back periodically to the teacher on their progress. One of the most famous koans is "What is the sound of one hand clapping?" Another is "What was your original face before your parents were born?" If you think these questions sound weird, inscrutable, or nonsensical, that's precisely the point. The tradition would tell you that you need to sit with them, let them sink in for a while, and let them do their work on you.

All three of these techniques—formless meditation, pointing-out instructions, and koans—are intended not to gradually settle and purify the mind in the way that mindfulness meditation might but rather to disrupt one's usual patterns of thinking. They hope to provoke a "breakthrough" realization whereby the practitioner recognizes the Awakeness that has always been there. However, it is often said that it's in fact not necessary to use a technique of any kind for such a breakthrough to occur. Huineng, for example, the illiterate victor of the poetry contest, is said to have Awakened when he was a young boy, while selling firewood to support his family. As he was making a delivery, he overheard someone chanting the *Diamond Sutra* (*Jingang Jing*) and suddenly realized his Buddha-nature. The trigger doesn't even have to be Buddhist per se: A popular story about a Zen temple servant named Chiyono, for example, recounts how her sudden Awakening happened when a bamboo pail she was carrying broke and spilled the water.

The aha moment of sudden Awakening is often referred to using the Japanese words *satori* or *kensho*. There have been many attempts to describe what this is like, but as is the case with all deeply spiritual or mystical experiences, it is exceedingly difficult to pin down in words. I would say that seeing your Buddha-nature is like suddenly realizing that the sights, sounds, and sensations you've been totally immersed in your whole life are actually a simulation or a virtual reality world that is created in your mind. You briefly pop out of that simulation and see how the mirage is being constructed by the mind. Your sense of being a "self" disappears instantaneously. What's left is a deep sense of all-pervasive emptiness or stillness, or an experience of oneness with all beings or with the entire universe. In this state, there is nothing to do, nowhere to go, no need to strive for anything at all. Everything is perfect just the way it is. You could live, die, or be reborn in a different body, but it wouldn't matter. Whatever might happen mentally or physically, you know that your Buddha-nature will be luminous, aware of everything, and perfectly at ease with all of it.

Mahayana Buddhists have spent much of the past two millennia describing, elaborating on, and speculating about these types of experiences (and for more information you can look into terms such as *rigpa*, *jnana*, *prajna*, and *tathagatagarbha*, or, in English, "nature of mind," "original mind," "awake awareness," and "direct knowing," in addition to Buddha-nature). However, be aware that every author who has ever written about Buddha-nature has said that it's impossible to communicate it clearly with words.

The reason that descriptions can't do it justice is that we are not talking about a conceptual thing but rather a firsthand realization. Think about it: Isn't it true that any first-person experience can never be fully conveyed by language? Even something as mundane as tasting a new flavor is an experience that can't be pinned down with words. Imagine trying to describe the flavor of a cup of coffee to someone who has never had one. The best you can do with words is to get them into the right neighborhood, based on their own previous experiences. "It's kind of like hot chocolate," you might say. "But more acidic and more earthy, and a lot more bitter."

Would they really understand what it's like to taste coffee from that description? No way! The only way to really know that experience is to just take a sip, and then it will all make sense instantaneously, without any need for language. As the famous Zen parable puts it, words are just fingers pointing at the moon. Don't just look at the finger; you need to look up and see the moon!

You might now be wondering whether this kind of mystical or spiritual breakthrough experience is actually real. Is seeing one's Buddha-nature seeing "reality as it is," or a myth, or a hallucinatory brain state? I promised at the outset that I'm not here to tell you what to think, and I certainly won't start doing so now. But, in my opinion, I don't think you can just dismiss accounts of this kind of experience outright. Whether or not you agree that these are insights into the true nature of the universe, it is clear that many humans have had these kinds of experiences and have found them to be incredibly meaningful, transformative, and life-changing.

I think that "realizing your Buddha-nature" is a particularly Buddhist way of describing a certain type of experience that is well within the realm of possibility for human beings. Mystics, philosophers, and poets throughout the world and across history have described breakthrough realizations, including the medieval German preacher Meister Eckhart (ca. 1260–1328); the Persian poet Rumi (thirteenth century); the transcendentalist author Ralph Waldo Emerson (1803–1882); the Hindu mystic Ramana Maharshi (1879–1950); contemporary spirituality authors like Douglas Harding, Eckhart Tolle, Byron Katie, or Joan Tollifson; and countless other writers from many other cultures. Each of them uses different words and metaphors, and each places their experiences within a different religious or spiritual framework, but it's clear to me that they are all trying to communicate experiences that belong in the same general category.

One way of talking about what these experiences have in common is to classify them as "non-dual." Religions and philosophies that are "dual" see an irreconcilable gulf between the ordinary world and the enlightened state, between the soul and God, between the self and the world, or between consciousness and matter. Non-dual systems, on the other hand, teach that these boundaries are illusory. In India, entire religions have been built up around the premise that you can unify the individual self—with all of its problems of anxiety, fear, sadness, helplessness, and self-identification—with a greater, cosmic, divine, wise, and perfect whole that encompasses all of reality. Such traditions include most forms of Hinduism and Buddhism.

However, there is one thing that separates Buddhism from many other non-dual traditions, both in India and beyond. That is its emphasis on using subtraction rather than addition to describe its non-dual insights. A non-dual form of Hinduism, such as Advaita Vedanta, says that an individual's soul merges or unites with God. Buddhism, on the other hand, generally prefers to describe this insight in the negative. The self is inherently illusory, it insists. There is no God with which to merge. Instead, our true inner nature is a vast, still emptiness.

While there is general agreement that this kind of non-dual insight is the key to basically all forms of Buddhism, there is disagreement about whether this realization should unfold gradually or happen suddenly, and whether it represents the end or the beginning of one's spiritual journey. Most forms of Buddhism, as I have been describing in previous chapters, teach that the dissolution of the self into Nirvana is the goal that comes at the end of a long quest to attain Awakening. In these forms of practice, the journey is essentially dualistic until the very end, because I am not Awakened and I am trying to acquire Awakening by walking the Path. In contrast, forms of Buddhism that talk about Buddha-nature are non-dual from the start. Awakening need not happen at the end of a long slog of trying to perfect oneself, because it's always here right now.

Nevertheless, even in forms of Buddhism that speak like this, it is not usually the case that once you see your Buddha-nature, you are instantaneously fully and perfectly enlightened and have no more work to do. It's a tremendously important insight and a wondrous experience, but, regardless, it is normally just the beginning of a long process of learning to abide in that perspective for more than a few moments at a time, to allow it to come to full bloom, and to embody it in all aspects of daily life. At the very least, though, once you have glimpsed your Buddha-nature, you know that Awakening is not "out there" somewhere. It is the paradoxical "pathless path" that's been right under your nose all along. Even closer than your nose. In fact, even closer than the breath inside your nose.

Uh-oh. Looks like I had better stop there, since it seems I've begun speaking in koans myself!

10

THE MIDDLE WAY

The "middle way" (also translated "middle path," *madhyama-pratipada*) is a term that was introduced early in Buddhist history. Originally, it referred to the compromise the Buddha made between extremes: living as a self-indulgent prince in a luxurious palace early in his life and, when he first went forth into the forest, starving himself and living a severely austere life in order to force a spiritual Awakening. In the end, they say, the Buddha discovered a middle ground. Like Goldilocks's porridge, the middle way he discovered is just right.

That's the original meaning of the middle way, but the term took on a completely different meaning in Mahayana Buddhism, and that's what concerns us here in this chapter. The Mahayana reinterpretation of the term gained popularity, mainly due to the Buddhist philosopher Nagarjuna, who lived around the second century CE. I'm not going to be able to do justice to all of his ideas here, but he is one of the towering giants, not just of Buddhist or Indian history but indeed of the global history of philosophy.

Nagarjuna famously stated that all objects and concepts are empty (*sunyata*). We have already discussed how, according to Buddhism, the self we carry around with us is not a thing but rather a feeling that's being constructed by our minds. Well, Nagarjuna showed that every other physical and mental object in the world—what Buddhists refer to as "forms"—can similarly be deconstructed. He did so by demonstrating that words are just concepts and do not point to independent, self-evident things.

For example, I'm writing this book on something called a laptop. You might think that a laptop is a specific and concrete object, but is it really? If we look closely, we find that this seemingly independent object is actually an assembly of glass, metal, and plastic components. If we broke down those components further, we'd find that they are in turn made up of individual molecules, then elements, atoms, and even subatomic particles. We could search and search, but we would never find the essence of laptopness in any of these pieces. We call an object a laptop when the parts are assembled in a particular way, but at the level of ultimate reality, a laptop isn't any more real than a self. These are both just conventional names we've decided to use to point to concepts. Buddhists signal the constructed nature of laptops, selves, and all other forms by calling them empty.

One branch of Buddhist philosophy, named Yogacara in Sanskrit but often called the Mind-Only school in English, denies that the universe of forms—the world of laptops, of objects and concepts, of selves and individuals—is real at all. According to this school, everything we can know is simply a representation in the mind. As in the movie *The Matrix*, we live inside a mirage we mistakenly think is reality. Nagarjuna didn't go to this extreme, but he offered instead what he called a middle way. He referred to the world of forms as "conventional truth" and referred to their emptiness as "ultimate truth." This teaching of two truths or two levels of truth opened up a way for later Buddhists to speak in highly paradoxical ways, asserting that everything is real and yet, simultaneously, that nothing is.

In East Asia, the typical way of putting this is to say that "form is empty" while "emptiness is form." A short text called the *Heart Sutra* (*Xinjing*) contains perhaps the most famous statement of this paradox. This text, composed in China by the seventh century CE, represents an attempt to boil down to its essence, or heart, all of the subtle detail from the voluminous Buddhist literature on emptiness (what Buddhists call "the perfection of wisdom"). It is consequently one of the shortest, densest, and most poetic statements of Buddhist philosophy ever written. The critical lines read:

> *Form is none other than Emptiness;*
> *Emptiness is none other than Form.*
> *Form simply is Emptiness;*
> *Emptiness simply is Form.*

Throughout East Asia today, the *Heart Sutra* is widely quoted, chanted in temples, and copied out on calligraphy scrolls. I think it is not an exaggeration to say that this is the most popular Buddhist text in the world. It is also one of the most radical, as it goes on to argue that the teachings of the Buddha, the Four Noble Truths, and even Awakening itself are ultimately empty concepts.

Two contradictory things are true simultaneously. . . . Even Awakening is empty . . . Is your brain hurting yet? Well, if so, that's kind of the point. These statements are intended to be paradoxical. Instead of limiting ourselves to abstract and philosophically complex statements, why don't we illustrate these ideas with a specific example from our own lives?

As I am writing this chapter, in summer of 2020, there have been a number of demonstrations and riots across the United States protesting the use of violence by the police and the repeated killing of unarmed Black people. The national discourse at this moment is centered on the issue of race. So let's examine how the middle way would apply to race, shall we?

If we strictly apply the ideas we've been discussing, we have no choice but to concede that "race" is as empty as all of the other concepts rattling about in our minds. Deconstructing this particular concept into its constituent components, Buddhists would argue that race is not a fixed feature of the universe. Race is an idea that was invented in a particular time and place in history. As we currently use the term, race is a label that is assigned based on a certain interpretation of how things are. It's part of one's identity; it's a way of thinking about oneself and others; and it's a way of categorizing people into different groups based on visible or cultural features. Race, that is to say, is a constructed concept that is used to describe the world of forms. So when one achieves Nirvana or glimpses one's Buddha-nature, race is seen to be illusory along with all the rest of the forms. Your non-self or your Buddha-nature is not a thing, and thus it cannot be labeled as Black, White, Asian or so forth. Race simply cannot be an ultimate truth by Nagarjuna's definition.

At the same time, though, let's be honest: race is obviously very real. These labels are applied to us from birth; they're recorded on official documents; they're used by our families and communities throughout our lives; and they inextricably shape our destiny. Race has a major influence on our psychology and our social interactions, on how we are perceived by others and how we see ourselves. In all too many ways, race influences our economic fate, our opportunities for social mobility, our health outcomes, how we are treated when the police pull us over, and many other aspects of our realities. Given all of that, to say that race isn't real seems quite insensitive, even racist. In other words, while race is not an ultimate truth in Buddhist terms, it's a conventional truth that governs many aspects of the world of forms in real and tangible ways.

I have noticed that some Buddhists subscribe to a one-sided view of this matter and say that because race is not an ultimate truth, it is therefore simply an illusion. In more extreme versions of this view, they argue that a good Buddhist should ignore matters of race, that paying any attention to these issues is a waste of precious time that could be spent realizing non-self or Nirvana. However, since Nagarjuna's time, if not earlier, Mahayana Buddhism has argued that this kind of exclusive focus on the emptiness side of the equation is deluded and dangerous. To avoid falling into the trap of an emptiness-only viewpoint, Mahayana calls for a middle way. We need to strike a balance by acknowledging that from the Awakened perspective, all forms are ultimately empty, while also appreciating that from the human perspective, the world of forms is simultaneously very real and has tangible consequences.

According to the Mahayana point of view, the key teaching that brings us out of an emptiness-only viewpoint and into this middle way is compassion. Compassion is widely talked about in all schools of Buddhism, but it is particularly in Mahayana that it is paired with emptiness as one of two bedrock principles. Do you remember that Mahayana means Great Vehicle? Mahayanists like to say that this metaphorical vehicle is a chariot with two wheels—wisdom and compassion (*prajna* and *karuna*)—and that both wheels need to be the same size and equally functional for the chariot to move forward rather than just going in circles. Mahayanists insist that Buddhists must integrate an understanding of the ultimate truth of emptiness with an equal measure of compassion for how all beings are affected by the conventional truths of form. The Great Vehicle has often criticized Buddhists who do not attempt this balance as adhering to an "Inferior Vehicle" (*Hinayana*).

Applying this notion of the middle way to the question of race means both clearly seeing that race is ultimately empty, while nevertheless remaining deeply concerned about how race affects people's lives. At the same time that we can clearly see race as a construct, we still can care about the fact that billions of human beings around the world are harmed by this construct every day. We can invest ourselves in understanding all the ways that this construct insidiously shapes society, our interactions with each other, and our understanding of ourselves. And we can engage in as many ways as possible to learn about this construct and to grow in our understanding of its visible and invisible effects on us, for the benefit of ourselves and others.

The same analysis we have done about race could also apply to any other characteristic of identity, such as gender, sexual orientation, ethnicity, and nationality. Because identity is such a charged subject, the balancing act of finding the middle way has sometimes been controversial among contemporary Buddhist communities in the United States. Many American meditation centers have begun creating special meditation groups for people of color, for LGBTQ+ practitioners, and for others who are typically marginalized in mainstream American society. Pushback against such accommodations has often centered on the argument that these identities and separate spaces are irrelevant to the goals of meditation and contradictory to the Buddhist teaching on non-self that is the purpose of the practice.

Of course, that is all quite true from an emptiness-only perspective. But from a middle way perspective, it is simultaneously also true that these meditation centers exist in a society where race, gender, and sexual orientation are categories that shape people's lives every moment of every day. From this viewpoint, creating welcoming spaces for groups that are often marginalized is a compassionate way of behaving and an obvious necessity for a meditation center in contemporary America.

What do you think about this controversy? For the record, I'm taking the middle way on this issue! But where do you stand? Can you see both sides with equal clarity? Can you live with the paradox, allowing both ultimate and conventional truths to be simultaneously true?

Engaging with issues like identity and diversity is increasingly becoming the norm—not just in Mahayana centers but across the whole spectrum of Buddhist organizations. One of the international leaders in this area has been Soka Gakkai International (SGI), a modern Buddhist organization with roots in Japan. With twelve million members in 192 countries, SGI is the most ethnically diverse Buddhist sect in the world. In the United States, this organization has for decades been particularly popular among African Americans and has attracted notable Black followers, such as Herbie Hancock and Tina Turner. Other organizations that have recently been very active in keeping issues of race on the front burner include Buddhist Peace Fellowship and East Bay Meditation Center in Oakland, California. High-profile Buddhist authors, teachers, and activists who grapple with issues of race include Jan Willis, Zenju Earthlyn Manuel, angel Kyodo williams, and Lama Rod Owens. While the impetus for this Buddhist social justice movement began in the United States, there are now parallels around the world.

It's not a stretch to say that social justice is now a normal feature of modern global Buddhism. I think that these efforts are going to continue to increase in importance in the foreseeable future and that these activist sanghas are making important and lasting contributions to the Buddhist tradition. While there are still some detractors who say that these issues are new-fangled distractions from the goal of Awakening, to me, it is clear that Buddhist social activism is in perfect keeping with the traditional Mahayana concept of the middle way. The Mahayana ideal has always been the practitioner who pursues the "perfection of wisdom" while also being engaged and active in the world. The perfected sages of this model do not remain aloof on some mountaintop or in some cave, perpetually absorbed in Nirvana. Rather, they are comfortable among people and active in society, participating to make positive change in everyday life for all.

One of the most famous illustrations of this ideal is the "Ten Ox-herding Pictures" from twelfth-century China. This series of paintings with accompanying poems and commentaries has been translated and revisited many times by Chinese, Japanese, and Western Zen teachers over the centuries. Essentially, it illustrates the quest of the practitioner as they discover meditative insight (symbolized in the paintings by an elusive ox), become more adept in this wisdom, integrate it into life, and realize Awakening. In the final image and poem, the ox is no longer there: meditation is no longer needed, because Awakening is now part of every moment of the practitioner's life. But the Awakened practitioner is not residing in some isolated hermitage. Rather, they are said to be "mingling with the people of the world," engaging with conventional reality in a way that benefits all beings.

To pick up this metaphor and run with it, you could say that we have spent the first half of this book examining the process of finding and taming the ox. I've introduced Buddhism's core teachings on how to liberate ourselves from delusion and suffering by deconstructing the self and the world of forms. We've reviewed the specific tools and concepts that enable us to do this—renunciation, the Eightfold Path, mindfulness, and other practices. These tools have all been geared toward realization of non-self, Nirvana, emptiness, and Buddha-nature. In this chapter, however, we have turned the corner by integrating ultimate and conventional truths. We will now start bringing this conversation back into the ordinary world, riding the ox back home, so to speak. The whole second half of this book will therefore be about how Buddhism has been applied to life in conventional reality, in the world of forms. Some of what I have to say in the second half of the book may sound contradictory to what I've said in the first half. As we go forward, though, bear in mind the distinction between ultimate truth and conventional truth, and remember that the middle way is always supposed to be paradoxical.

11

SKILLFUL MEANS

I f you have been feeling that our trajectory over the last few chapters
has been too philosophical, you'll be happy to hear that it's time to
plant our feet back on the ground and to refocus our attention on the
ordinary world.

We've already discussed Mahayana's critique of what they call "Inferior Vehicle" priorities: that there can be far too much focus placed
on impermanence, non-self, Nirvana, and meditation at the expense
of compassionate engagement in life and society. However, it is not
accurate to say that all non-Mahayana Buddhism focuses completely
on emptiness to the exclusion of the world. In fact, there are examples
of Buddhist engagement with so-called worldly matters going all the
way back to scriptures written down in the first century BCE.

Although most of the Theravada Buddhist scriptures represent
teachings for the community of monks and nuns who had gone forth,
the Dharma is not just a set of teachings for ascetic renunciates. The
Buddha is also said to have taught all kinds of laypeople, from kings
to merchants to artisans. When he did so, he is said to have exhibited
"skillful means" (upaya, also called "expedient means"). This means
that he was always able to say exactly what the person he was addressing needed to hear, and it always made perfect sense to them, no
matter what their level of spiritual development.

Buddhist teachings for wider audiences tend not to emphasize philosophical or mystical doctrines about meditation and Awakening but instead revolve around themes of morality, karma, and compassion. When addressing kings, for example, the Buddha talks about how they could become "wheel-turning" monarchs (*cakravartin*). A ruler could learn to be righteous, generous, and benevolent; a father-figure and role model for his people; and a generous supporter of the Buddhist order.

The ruler who is usually held up as the best example of a wheel-turner is King Ashoka. In chapter 4, in our discussion of karma, we saw King Ashoka lose his power and wealth and yet donate his last worthy possession, a piece of medicinal fruit, to the sangha. While the story is legendary, there is historical evidence that King Ashoka existed. He is the ruler who first united India into a single empire in the third century BCE. According to historians, the real King Ashoka likely supported a number of religions throughout his realm. However, in Buddhist legends, he is credited with single-handedly spreading Buddhism throughout India and beyond.

In addition to teachings intended for rulers, there are also many for ordinary householders. One such text is the *Discourse to Sigala* (*Sigalovada Sutta*). In this story, a layman named Sigala had been performing a ritual to the six directions every morning. The Buddha suggests to him that, instead of engaging in this mechanical sort of religious devotion, he put his heart into six kinds of beneficial relationships. The Buddha outlines how he should treat his parents, his teacher, his spouse, his friends, his employees, and his spiritual mentors with virtue, kindness, and consideration, and then describes how those other people will reciprocate positively. This same text also advises the householder to avoid vices, to be frugal with money, and other general ethical teachings.

Perhaps the most common advice for getting along in everyday life found in Buddhist texts is a set of ten virtues that they say all people—monastic and lay—should be working on cultivating. These ten "perfections" (*paramita*) include generosity, morality, renunciation, wisdom, diligence, patience, honesty, determination, loving kindness, and equanimity. We already mentioned the Five Precepts for laypeople in chapter 4, which are considered the bare minimum requirements for a moral life that won't result in horrible karmic repercussions. These ten perfections set a higher bar. They are said to be the qualities that are exhibited by Awakened beings, and they are also virtues that you must perfect before it's possible for you to become Awakened. I have often heard Buddhist laypeople say that they don't have the inclination to meditate in this lifetime but that they are practicing the perfections in order to be reborn in a better circumstance so they can ordain as a monk and practice more seriously in the next lifetime.

While the teachings for kings, the stories about Ashoka, the discourse to Sigala, and the cultivation of the ten perfections are addressed to wider audiences, these Theravada doctrines still maintain a clear line between everyday life and the pursuit of Awakening. Theravada Buddhism preserves a fundamental dichotomy between "worldly" things (objects, actions, behaviors, and attitudes that are intended to help people get along in everyday life) and the "otherworldly" things (everything associated with renunciation, meditation, impermanence, non-self, and Nirvana). The Buddha repeats again and again throughout the scriptures that those who have gone forth should concentrate strictly on the otherworldly and ignore the worldly. He forbids monks and nuns from dancing, listening to music, enjoying entertainment, adorning themselves with flowers, wearing makeup and jewelry, and from even touching money. (They must rely on resident laypeople to handle financial affairs on their behalf.) He also forbids them from engaging in activities such as healing, astrology, fortune-telling, and a number of other activities that he deemed too worldly. Throughout history, these rules were frequently broken, but the prohibition is doctrinally important nonetheless.

In contrast, Mahayana Buddhism decisively rejects the idea of a dichotomy between worldly and otherworldly. They call this either/or division in early Buddhism yet another example of "Inferior Vehicle" thinking. As you might predict from our discussion in the previous chapter, Mahayana instead seeks to forge a middle way that balances worldly and otherworldly activities. Anything that is not directly related to the ultimate truth of Awakening yet benefits beings on the level of conventional truth could in the Mahayana be called skillful means. Since the Mahayana demands the full integration of ultimate and conventional truth, skillful means are considered an integral, indispensable part of Buddhist practice by this tradition.

This difference of opinion about Buddhist participation in worldly endeavors may at first seem like a minor doctrinal debate, but taking this expanded definition of skillful means seriously has led Mahayanists to completely reimagine what Buddhist practice is all about. According to the Theravada viewpoint, the only serious practitioners of the Buddha's teachings are those who have gone forth into the monastery—or laypeople living a quasi-monastic lifestyle focused on meditation. From the Mahayana viewpoint, however, serious practitioners of Buddhism can be found both inside and outside the monastery, and their practice of the Dharma is not necessarily directly tied to meditation. Anyone who is providing any kind of benefit for other beings, whether they are operating on the level of ultimate truth or conventional truth, is practicing the Dharma. Relating well to other people, managing a household well, ruling a kingdom well, and running a business well—if done with compassion for other beings—are all seen as critical parts of the practice of Buddhism.

The reframing I'm talking about also involved a dramatic change in the status of laypeople in Mahayana writings. In previous traditions, scriptures nearly always related stories about the Buddha or one of his monastic disciples. Laypeople play a limited role in these texts, primarily as followers, interlocutors, or foils for the Buddha. By contrast, laypeople are the central characters of some of the most iconic and influential scriptures in the Mahayana tradition. They are not tangential bit players in these stories, but fully enlightened models of wisdom and compassion and teachers of the Dharma par excellence.

The most famous example of an enlightened layperson is Vimalakirti, the hero of a theatrical Mahayana scripture called *Instructions of Vimalakirti* (*Vimalakirtinirdesa Sutra*). The story says that, although

he was never a monk, Vimalakirti has attained Awakening equivalent to a Buddha's and that he has gained perfect insight into the
ultimate truth of the emptiness of all things. What is fun about this
particular text is how the protagonist demonstrates his perfect understanding of emptiness through trickery, jokes, displays of magical
powers, and other feats. While behaving in this highly engaging and
entertaining way, he outwits and bedazzles a series of senior disciples
of the Buddha, various deities, and other model teachers. Often, the
brunt of Vimalakirti's jokes is the monk Sariputra, a senior disciple of
the Buddha, who in this text is represented as a buffoonish stickler for
the conservatism of the "Inferior Vehicle."

Another Mahayana scripture with an equally high estimation of
laypeople is the *Flower Ornament Scripture (Avatamsaka Sutra)*. A
lengthy chapter of this epic text recounts the pilgrimage of a seeker
named Sudhana, who travels near and far searching for teachers of
the Dharma. (This journey is featured in stone carvings on the walls
of Borobudur, the largest Buddhist temple in the world, built in Indonesia from the eighth to ninth century CE.) All in all, Sudhana is instructed by over fifty teachers. This list includes deities, monks, nuns,
scholars, and meditation masters. But he is also tutored by kings,
queens, householders, artisans, and children. He learns from a sailor,
a slave, and even a courtesan. The obvious point is that absolutely
anyone can be respected as a teacher of the Dharma.

When Sudhana meets with lay teachers in the *Flower Ornament
Scripture*, he is often shown how the practice of a particular profession or worldly activity can, in fact, be a skillful means for practicing
the Dharma in the conventional world. In the scene in which he is
instructed by a wealthy man, for example, Sudhana learns frugality;
from a healer, he learns compassion for the sick. When he meets with
the courtesan Vasumitra, she explains to him that her clients come to
her with their minds full of lust but that she uses this sexual impulse
to teach them freedom from passion. Sometimes, she says, they learn
this lesson from just looking at her, sometimes by embracing her, and
sometimes even by kissing her.

I think the story of a courtesan teaching the Dharma through sexuality would strike most non-Mahayana Buddhists—celibate monastics in particular and especially an uptight moralist conservative like Sariputra—as downright scandalous. But the Mahayana concept of skillful means allows for almost infinite leeway in the methods of instruction. In fact, Mahayanists are given permission to break even the most fundamental Buddhist rules of ethics in the service of skillful means. In the *Lotus Sutra* (*Saddharmapundarika Sutra*), one of the most influential Mahayana scriptures of all time, the Buddha explains skillful means by comparing himself to a father who lies to his children in order to entice them to do the right thing. If the Buddha can lie, then pretty much anything goes! But—and this is a big but—it's only legitimately considered skillful means if it brings benefit and does no harm. The whole point of skillful means is that it seeks to mitigate suffering and maximize well-being for all.

This expansion of skillful means I have been talking about in this chapter didn't just change Mahayana Buddhist philosophy and scripture; it also radically transformed the ways that Mahayana Buddhists have engaged in real-life social, political, and cultural activities. It is the reason that Mahayana practitioners and organizations have always been involved in outreach, charity, and socially engaged work in the public sphere.

To illustrate, when I spent a year and half as a visiting scholar at a Buddhist monastic university in Taiwan while writing my PhD dissertation, I visited a Mahayana Buddhist humanitarian organization, the Tzu Chi (Compassionate Relief) Foundation, which is headquartered on the eastern coast of Taiwan. With branches in more than fifty countries, the foundation specializes in community service, medical aid, recycling, and disaster relief. Among their many initiatives, they have built hospitals in Taiwan and in many countries around the world. Several years later, while I was in Los Angeles, I had the opportunity to visit one of their charitable medical clinics, which regularly provides free medical assistance to the local community, as well as to migrant workers in the agricultural areas around the city.

Tzu Chi is, I think, a perfect example of how the Mahayana idea of skillful means inspires Buddhists to get involved with social action on a mass scale. The organization was founded in 1968 by a nun named Cheng Yen (b. 1937) and initially focused on collecting donations from local lay members in order to provide assistance to the poor in eastern Taiwan. As it grew, more and more volunteers became associated with Tzu Chi, until it reached its current size of over ten million members. That membership is virtually all laypeople, some of whom are financial donors and some of whom are doctors or other professionals who also donate their time and expertise. While Tzu Chi does organize some devotional activities for its members, such as chanting services and other ceremonies, the majority of the organization's activities are of a worldly nature. The purpose of the organization, some of its leaders told me in an interview, is to give volunteers the opportunity to engage in skillful means, practicing Buddhism by making a difference in the world.

Tzu Chi is a paradigmatic example of what has commonly been called "engaged Buddhism," or in Chinese *renjian fojiao*, "humanistic Buddhism." These are terms that emphasize the integration of Buddhism with charity, social work, environmental activism, social justice, and other aspects of everyday life. Buddhists have always been engaged in society, but this represents a major trend in twentieth- and twenty-first-century Buddhism. Engaged Buddhism is mainly fueled by the Mahayana ethos of using skillful means to alleviate the suffering of all beings everywhere; however, these days, the drive to get involved socially is so strong that many Theravada Buddhist organizations have also become involved.

So, yes, the stereotype that Buddhists are a bunch of totally detached navel-gazers has sometimes been well-earned. However, the number of Buddhist meditators who are holed up in a cave or on a mountaintop somewhere perpetually absorbed in meditation is dwarfed by the number of engaged Buddhist laypeople who are out there making the world a better place through skillful means. In any event, according to the doctrine of the middle way, we need both kinds of people involved in both kinds of activities in order to keep the chariot's two wheels rolling forward. As the audacious trickster Vimalakirti put it in the text that bears his name: we need wisdom to liberate the full potential of our skillful means and skillful means to liberate the full potential of our wisdom.

12

BODHISATTVA

Before you whip out your air guitar and start playing along, let me warn you that this chapter has nothing to do with the Steely Dan song! The word "bodhisattva" means something like "Awakened essence." A bodhisattva is a Buddha-to-be, someone on their way to becoming a Buddha.

In the Theravada tradition, in which there is only one Buddha per aeon and that role has already been filled during this current aeon by Siddhartha Gautama, the word simply refers to him before he became Awakened. In Mahayana, on the other hand, there are countless buddhas in countless Pure Lands strewn across the cosmos, making possible an infinite number of bodhisattvas. The word therefore is used liberally to refer to any Buddhist practitioner who is on the Path toward Buddhahood—no matter how many more lifetimes they have to go before they get there.

In a text called *Graduated Dharma-Gates Explicating the Perfection of Meditation* (*Shi chanboluomi cidi famen*), the founder of the Chinese school of Tian Tai Buddhism Zhiyi (538–597) introduced what came to be called the "four bodhisattva vows." These vows became extremely popular and are chanted aloud as daily reminders of what it means to be a bodhisattva in many Buddhist monasteries and meditation centers across East Asia today. These four sentences provide a pithy outline of the core mission of Mahayana Buddhist practice:

> *Innumerable sentient beings:*
>   *I vow to save them all.*
> *Inexhaustible afflictions:*
>   *I vow to break them all.*
> *Infinite Dharma Gates:*
>   *I vow to learn them all.*
> *The unsurpassable Way of the Buddhas:*
>   *I vow to accomplish it all.*

As you can see, these vows are a far cry from a sole focus on personal liberation from duhkha. Their agenda is truly staggering: the Mahayana practitioner vows to save (i.e., Awaken) all of the beings in the universe, to overcome any and all afflictions, to learn an infinite number of practices that lead to Awakening, and to achieve full Buddhahood.

Of course, it would be impossible to accomplish all of this in a single lifetime, but Mahayanists are prepared for the long haul. Many Buddhists would like to become Awakened in one lifetime, to dissolve into Nirvana at the moment of death and end the cycle of rebirths. But for Mahayanists, that would be considered an "Inferior Vehicle" goal, a selfish and limited implementation of Buddhist teachings. The Great Vehicle alternative is to accomplish Awakening while remaining within the cycle of samsara. A model Mahayana bodhisattva is so wise that they can transcend rebirth if they so desire yet so compassionate that they choose to come back again and again in order to help, to teach, and to remove the suffering of all beings they encounter lifetime after lifetime. They vow to delay their own salvation in order to stay in the world until every last being in the universe is Awakened. This all-for-one-and-one-for-all mindset is called *bodhicitta*, the "Awakening mind."

I think this is a beautiful sentiment. Idealistic but lovely. I can see how, for members of the Tzu Chi Foundation and other Buddhist charities, thinking of themselves as bodhisattvas would be enormously inspirational. Aside from calling Buddhists into a life of service, though, there are other implications of the idea of the bodhisattva that I want to focus on in this chapter. Many schools of Mahayana imagine that, in addition to ordinary bodhisattvas such as the millions of members of Tzu Chi, there are also some individuals out there who have cultivated wisdom, compassion, the perfections, and skillful means for countless lifetimes. Bodhisattvas come in degrees, and some bodhisattvas have achieved the highest levels of attainment, becoming godlike beings in the process.

We discussed the Mahayana view of the cosmos in chapter 7. With multiple Pure Lands in all directions and multiple buddhas manifesting multiple bodies across the universe, it gets complicated rather quickly. What I didn't mention in chapter 7 is that there is also a whole retinue of powerful celestial bodhisattvas who are constantly moving back and forth between these different worlds. If it is helpful, you might think of them as roughly equivalent to angels or saints in Christianity: their job is to keep watch over the universe and to come to the assistance of anyone who calls upon them wherever they may be.

Historically in Mahayana cultures, particular celestial bodhisattvas have been popular objects of devotion. In fact, their popularity often eclipses that of the buddhas. The most popular of these bodhisattvas include Ksitigarbha, whose name means Womb of the Earth and who is said to have traveled to the underworld in order to release all the beings trapped in the hell realms. Most East Asian temples have an altar dedicated to him that serves as a place for memorial plaques, flowers, and offerings for the deceased. Another popular figure is Mañjusri, the bodhisattva of wisdom, who is recognizable by the flaming sword he bears in one hand, symbolizing his ability to cut away delusion. He usually also carries a Buddhist scripture, indicating the source of his great wisdom. A third popular bodhisattva,

Maitreya, is slated to become the next Buddha of our own world. Currently living in a paradise realm called Tusita, he will appear here once the Dharma has been forgotten and needs rediscovering in the next aeon. Incidentally, Budai, the Chinese Santa Claus from chapter 7, supposedly is a manifestation of Maitreya. So, he's not a buddha, but he is a bodhisattva.

While these three notable bodhisattvas are indeed important, the most popular Mahayana deity of all is Avalokitesvara, known in Chinese as Guanyin, in Tibetan as Chenrezig, and in Japanese as Kannon. Avalokitesvara is considered a universal savior deity. His name literally means Lord Who Looks Down or Perceiving the Sounds of the World, depending on which language you are translating from. In English, Avalokitesvara is frequently referred to as the Bodhisattva of Compassion, the Bodhisattva of Mercy, or other similar terms. Avalokitesvara is introduced in one of the most popular and well-circulated Mahayana Buddhist scriptures of all time, the *Lotus Sutra*. In that text, the bodhisattva pledges to come to the rescue of any and all people who call upon him for assistance. He specifically mentions overcoming floods, shipwrecks, demons, bandits, and a number of other disasters, as well as helping to overcome greed, anger, and ignorance. He says that he will appear in whatever form would be helpful at that particular moment, be it a buddha, a god, a king, any type of monastic or layperson, a child, a spirit, or any other sentient being.

Being a shapeshifter who can take on different forms, Avalokitesvara is depicted in artwork in a variety of ways. Early statues of this deity usually portray a prince adorned with jeweled clothing, an elaborate headdress, and other ornaments. In some cultures, he is shown with a horse's head or as a wild-eyed demon with fangs. The most common depiction in Chinese-speaking cultures is as a white-robed female figure who looks somewhat similar to the Virgin Mary. In Tibetan Buddhism, the female manifestation of Avalokitesvara is named Tara, and she is depicted with skin that is white, green, red, or other colors, each symbolizing a different meaning.

These female forms of Avalokitesvara are especially popular among women across the Buddhist world. In female form, the bodhisattva is understood as a mother goddess, and Mahayanists often pray to her for help with women's health issues—successful pregnancy and safe childbirth in particular. It is common for female devotees to wear a jade or crystal amulet of the deity's image around their necks, which is meant to protect them from bad luck or any other catastrophes.

Whether depicted as male or female, or sometimes in a nonbinary "middle way" in-between the two, Avalokitesvara is often depicted with a thousand arms extending in all directions, each hand holding a different implement or tool that can be used to help people in need. In addition to a thousand arms, there are often also eleven heads, all stacked on top of each other, in order to ensure that anyone who needs help throughout the cosmos is seen and heard. (Incidentally, if you've never seen it, take a moment to Google the "Thousand Hand Dance" by the China Disabled People's Performing Art Troupe. It's amazing, and there's even one version of the performance set to the Steely Dan song!)

Given that Avalokitesvara is believed to be so attentive to those who are suffering and so capable of coming to their assistance, devotees are apt to interpret any unexpected positive intervention in their lives as being due to the deity. If someone randomly did something that helped you out of a bind or that helped you to avert some misfortune or another, then you might think that you had been visited by Avalokitesvara, who had momentarily taken the form of that person. I once was told by a high-level official within the Tzu Chi Foundation that the members and volunteers of the humanitarian organization are none other than Avalokitesvara's hands. As they assist suffering beings in the midst of disaster and illness, they think of themselves both as bodhisattvas in their own right and also as Avalokitesvara's helpers carrying out his vows to leave no sentient being uncared for.

In addition to momentarily appearing disguised as a helpful person, Avalokitesvara is also said to be regularly born on earth in a manifestation body—one of the three bodies of a Buddha I mentioned in chapter 7, or, in this case, one of the bodies of a perfectly Awakened bodhisattva. A manifestation body is a physical body that seemingly is born, lives, and dies on earth in human form, but it is actually a projection or materialization of an Awakened being.

In the Tibetan language, this kind of manifestation body is called a *tulku*. There are multiple tulku lineages active in contemporary Tibetan culture. When one person in a tulku lineage dies, a search begins for the next incarnation. Usually, the next person is identified while quite young, based on a number of signs, oracles, or seemingly miraculous coincidences. The child who has been identified is usually taken to a monastery to be raised within a highly ritualized environment, and they grow up being treated by Tibetan Buddhists as a god incarnate.

Perhaps you already know one of the most famous examples of a tulku, a Tibetan monk named Tenzin Gyatso. He was born in 1940 in a particularly important tulku lineage, that of the Dalai Lamas. Being recognized as the fourteenth Dalai Lama makes him both the head of the Gelugpa branch of Tibetan Buddhism and also the nominal political leader of Tibet. Dalai Lamas are also considered to be manifestation bodies of—yes, you guessed it—the bodhisattva Avalokitesvara. This is a tradition that is many centuries old, which holds that Avalokitesvara continually reincarnates himself as wise and compassionate leaders in order to protect and guide the Tibetan people.

In 1959, when he was still quite young, the Fourteenth Dalai Lama fled the violent occupation of his homeland by the Chinese military, and he established a Tibetan exile community in northern India. This has made him something of an international symbol of the plight of the Tibetan people and of the oppression of traditional culture under Communism. It has also made him an ongoing target of scorn of the Chinese government and its sympathizers. Despite their attempts to discredit him—or perhaps *because* of them—the Dalai Lama has become a familiar face in the West and around the world. I'd say he is the most famous living Buddhist today, by a long shot.

The Dalai Lama has been a major proponent of overcoming sectarianism and promoting interfaith dialogue, and he has engaged in or organized many high-level talks, conferences, and gatherings dedicated to global peace and religious tolerance. He was awarded a Nobel Peace Prize for these efforts in 1989. He has also been active in dialogues between Buddhism and science, playing a major role in inspiring research into the medical benefits of meditation. The Dalai Lama has released many books, recordings, and YouTube videos in English on all sorts of topics related to Buddhism, all of which are broadly accessible and widely popular. As a result—while he is not a pope or an archbishop of Buddhism and is not even the leader of all orders of Tibetan Buddhism—this particular Dalai Lama does in many ways act as the de facto global spokesperson for Buddhism.

So what is the message that this famous Buddhist spokesperson and manifestation body of the Bodhisattva of Compassion would like to deliver to the world? He has done a lot of work in a lot of different arenas, but he has stated many times that the core of his teaching is simply kindness. He has frequently stressed that this is the most important virtue, over and above all other teachings of Buddhism. In his book *The Dalai Lama: A Policy of Kindness*, for example, he describes his approach succinctly: "This is my simple religion. There is no need for temples; no need for complicated philosophy. Our own brain, our own heart is our temple; the philosophy is kindness."

Although the Dalai Lama himself often downplays his own importance, saying that he's "just a simple monk," I ask you, if Avalokitesvara really were to manifest himself here on earth in human form, wouldn't his message be precisely that?

13

COMPASSION

I've mentioned compassion many times over the past three chapters. It is a paramount virtue in Mahayana, but all forms of Buddhism have a lot to say on this theme. Let's dive into the subject. But first we should define our terms.

Buddhists tend to be much more precise about compassion than we usually are in everyday English. We commonly use the word in rather vague ways, to refer to a whole range of positive feelings. Buddhists, on the other hand, differentiate between four different positive mental states that might all be part of the ordinary English notion of compassion. Collectively known as the "immeasurable states of mind" (*si wuliang xin*) in Chinese or the "heavenly dwellings" (*brahma vihara*) in Pali, they are as follows:

- Loving kindness (*metta* in Pali): a feeling of universal friendliness, goodwill, and love toward all beings.
- Empathetic compassion (*karuna*): a feeling of wanting to remove the suffering experienced by other beings.
- Altruistic joy (*mudita*): a feeling of joy at the happiness and success of other beings, untinged by jealousy or pride.
- Equanimity (*upekkha*): a feeling of tolerance, peace, and tranquility in the face of annoyances, including those caused by other beings.

These four immeasurables were understood to go together as a set in Indian culture long before the Buddha's time, and they appear in other Indian religious traditions as well. However, they were absorbed into Buddhism and came to be among its central ideas. The main idea behind the Buddhist discourses on this subject is that we can and should cultivate these positive states of mind. As is true with mindfulness or concentration, the brain can be trained in the immeasurables.

Predictably, different forms of Buddhism have taught different ways to practice this training. One of the best-known ways in Western Buddhist circles is a sequence popularized by Sharon Salzberg in her book *Lovingkindness: The Revolutionary Art of Happiness.* You start by directing positivity toward yourself, repeating phrases such as "May I be happy," "May I be well," "May I abide in well-being," or any other phrase or set of phrases that are similarly friendly and kind. After a time, you branch out to the people around you whom you care for ("May they be happy," etc.). You then expand the circle to dwell in loving kindness for all the people in the world whom you don't know, and you finish by spreading it to those with whom you have a more complicated or antagonistic relationship.

A different way of arriving at the same place is to imagine you are projecting positive vibrations out in all directions. From my location here in Philadelphia, for example, I might imagine my goodwill extending eastward across the Atlantic and onward to Europe, Northern Africa, the Middle East, and beyond. I can then visualize sending my friendliness to the west, then to the north and south, until I have covered the whole world. Yet another way is to spread your kind thoughts throughout the levels of rebirth, from people down to animals, ghosts, and hell-beings, and then up to the angelic beings and the gods. (Notice the difference between praying to gods asking them to make you happy versus simply wishing them well.)

Whatever way you follow this practice, the basic idea is the same: you intentionally try to generate beneficial states of mind and direct these toward yourself and other beings. From the perspective of a strictly emptiness-only interpretation of reality, this practice appears superfluous. Thoughts are illusions, right? Selves are constructs, right? Why, then, would I waste time intentionally generating thoughts and directing them toward these selves? Most Buddhists would readily agree that this practice is not geared toward ultimate truth or Awakening, that it will not bring you a realization of "reality as it is." However, from the perspective of conventional truth, this practice is extremely important. Training in the immeasurables is the foundation for skillful means and for engaged Buddhism, and it is the very heart of the bodhisattva Path.

Part of the power of this kind of practice is that it has the ability to disrupt the loops of unkind, negative, and self-destructive thoughts toward ourselves and others that most of us normally hear playing inside our heads. If the thoughts floating down your mindstream are angry, for example, the perfect antidote may be to fill your mind up with loving kindness instead. If your thoughts tend toward cruelty or violence, why not replace them with empathetic compassion? If your thoughts often revolve around jealousy or greed, perhaps balance them with altruistic joy. If your mind is characteristically annoyed or perturbed by the people around you, then try to cultivate a little equanimity. Even if you recognize that this practice involves artificially creating positive affirmations and even if you know you are intentionally planting them in your head, it can still work. In fact, it can still work even if you don't actually feel anything while you are saying these words—even if your repetitions are completely mechanical.

I'll tell you a personal story to illustrate: Remember how several chapters back I mentioned that I spent a summer as a resident in a Theravada monastery in Thailand? Well, I went there after five years of intensive meditation practice focused on realizing Nirvana. I felt like I was burning out on it, getting way too goal-focused, and becoming increasingly detached from the people around me. I had gone to the monastery with the intention to experience renunciation, but the longer I stayed, the more I realized that I wanted to be more fully engaged with the world. I didn't know the Mahayana concept of the middle way at the time, but looking back I would say that I had become fixated on an emptiness-only approach to life. When I sought meditation guidance from a senior meditation teacher, the monk convinced me to try a new practice that consisted of repeating phrases of loving kindness.

At first I thought this practice was ridiculous. Do you remember the *Saturday Night Live* skit "Daily Affirmation with Stuart Smalley"? (If you know who J. P. Sears is, this was basically the 1990s equivalent.) Well, I felt as cheesy as Stuart Smalley repeating these silly little affirmations. It seemed pointless and not at all like the serious meditation I was used to. I was reluctant, but I had asked for direction and had been given this new practice, so I decided to trust the monk and give it a try.

There was a lot of work to be done around the monastery during the rainy season, and there was a lot less time dedicated to intensive sitting meditation than I had expected. I was assigned a number of different jobs on different days, but the thing I did more than anything else was sweep the dirt paths around the monastery grounds. This particular monastery was located in a remote rainforest in far eastern Thailand. The grounds were covered with trees, and leaves were constantly falling onto the dirt paths. In the rainforest, this can be quite dangerous, as all sorts of insects and small animals hide under the leaves. To avoid stepping on them, thereby either killing them or getting bitten by them, it's best both for the humans and for the insects not to let the leaves lie on the paths. That summer, for hours on end, I walked the grounds with a broom, sweeping the paths clear. It was a never-ending task: the leaves fell so fast that as soon as I got to the end of the paths, I had to start again at the beginning.

As I was sweeping day after day, I did my recitations in synch with my movements. Each time my broom swept across the ground, I repeated a phrase: "May I be happy." Sweep. "May I be well." Sweep. I repeated that a bunch of times, and then moved on to the next phrase: "May all of us here be happy." Sweep. "May all of us here be well." Sweep. Repeat. "May all beings everywhere be happy." Sweep. "May all beings everywhere be well." Sweep. Repeat. Then, at the end of the whole cycle, start again from the top. Over and over again, all day, all summer long, repeating those same phrases.

Before I continue this story, let me ask you: What do you predict would happen to you if you did this? How do you think your own mind would respond to several months of intensive reprogramming? Initially, I thought it was silly and boring, but it didn't take more than a few days for these phrases to stop feeling strange. You know what it's like to get a song stuck in your head. Well, soon enough, these phrases were playing in my head all day and all night without any effort on my part to remember to do it. By the end of a month, they increasingly crowded out my other thoughts. I remember thinking at the time that it was as if I had ejected a CD that had been playing in my head with all my usual random monkey-mind chatter and popped in another CD that only played one track of loving kindness, on repeat forever. (For all you Gen Z readers, yes, this was back in the '90s when we still had that ancient technology!)

Eventually, as the weeks went on, something started to happen that surprised me even more. The rote repetition of these statements started to become increasingly meaningful. They were no longer just a repetitive loop of words, but rather they started to open up a new range of emotion. I would be out on the path, sweeping away, and I would suddenly feel overcome by a strong sense of tranquility and peacefulness, a sense that I and all the creatures around me in the forest were in perfect harmony. When I came across an insect under a leaf, I would be filled with concern for its well-being, treating it with the utmost care as I removed it from the path. When I heard a tropical bird sing, I would be filled with a sense of joy at its happy sound. If a person came up the path while I was sweeping, I would experience waves of loving kindness for them. How could my heart be opening like this from the repetition of a bunch of silly words?

The clincher occurred one evening when I attended the mandatory evening meeting with the other residents of the monastery. These hour-long chanting and meditation sessions were held in a building with Thai-style architecture, meaning there were no walls. If you've ever been in the tropics, you know that that means mosquitoes. The whole lot of us—all the monks and other monastery residents like me—would get eaten alive every night. I would routinely get a dozen or more mosquito bites every evening and spent each session ruminating about all the mosquito-borne diseases I was probably exposing myself to: dengue fever, malaria, who knows what else. These evening sessions caused me quite a bit of stress, and I dreaded them.

One night, though, there I was in the evening meeting right in the middle of my meditation on the immeasurables when a mosquito landed on my arm. I felt its presence and opened my eyes, looking down as it started to suck my blood. Normally, the annoyance and anxiety would have started up. But this time, I was instead surprised by a feeling of kindness toward the mosquito. The thought came to me that this was a living being who was looking to feed her hungry family. She only needed a small amount of blood from me, and she must have been happy to have found such an abundant source of food. I began to also feel compassion for myself: I had been generating so much anxiety about this, but I could see in that moment that I was actually okay with the situation. *Metta, karuna, mudita, upekkha.*

Let's be clear: I'm not saying that you should run outside right this moment and sacrifice yourself to whatever hungry animals are out there. (Although, come to think of it, there are quite a few jataka stories about the Buddha in previous lives doing precisely that.) I am also not saying that I'm some kind of saintly figure who has mastered compassion. In fact, I have never been as single-mindedly engaged in the practice of the immeasurables as I was that summer, and I have never been able to maintain that intense level of compassion again. I'm sorry to say that I've swatted many hungry mosquitoes since then.

The simple point I want to emphasize is that, just as the mind can be trained to concentrate more and more through the practice of mindfulness meditation, it can also be trained to become more and more kind, compassionate, and even-keeled through meditation practice focused on the immeasurables. There isn't any magic woo-woo going on here. From what we know about the neuroplasticity of the brain, it is not at all surprising that we can transform anger, anxiety, and self-concern into gentleness, calm, and generosity toward others if we are willing to commit the time to the practice of reprogramming ourselves.

On the other hand, Buddhists like to tell all kinds of tales about the power of the immeasurables, as if compassion does give you magical powers. They especially like stories that feature the instant defeat of fear and enmity. For example, there's a famous legend that involves a drunken and enraged elephant charging at the Buddha and a number of other people nearby. While pandemonium immediately breaks out among the crowd, the Buddha calmly projects loving kindness directly at the elephant, reaching out to stroke its forehead. The elephant is immediately subdued, kneeling and bowing before the Buddha. That story is from the scriptures, but I've also heard many similar Thai yarns involving famous monks subduing aggressive tigers or bandits or assassins or other foes.

I don't know if the immeasurables really could halt an attack on your life that way, but I would wager that they could definitely help you better deal with some of the problematic people in your life. It's not easy to feel kindness, compassion, joy, or equanimity for those who have harmed you without getting hung up on questions like "Does she deserve my compassion?" or "Can I ever forgive him?" It feels difficult to even think about forgiveness, as if your heart is cold and closed off. You feel as though you can't move past your disappointment and you don't want to let go of your anger.

But the lesson I took from sweeping in the forest was that those hesitations don't actually matter. Never mind how it feels right now: If you just repeat the phrases mechanically, like a CD track stuck on repeat, you soon find your existing mental patterns getting reprogrammed despite yourself. Where you once had anger, resentment, or fear, these eventually transform into kindness, care, joy, and equanimity. The feeling of being closed off starts to loosen its hold. You won't necessarily become best friends with your former enemy, and you might not be any closer to the ultimate truth of "reality as it is." But you certainly can come to feel more at ease with the difficult situations in your life. And that in and of itself is a powerful form of skillful means, wouldn't you say?

14

RITUALS

As a professor who teaches college courses on Buddhism, one of my favorite ways to start off a new semester is to ask students what they think Buddhism is. My students most commonly argue that it is a philosophy or a way of life and resist the idea that it is a religion. On the last day of the semester, once they have actually learned a bit about Buddhism, we revisit this question, and they almost universally have come around to seeing it primarily as a religion. It's not yet the end of our tour of Buddhism's most important ideas, but let me ask you: As of right now, where do you stand on this question?

In my opinion, your answer says more about you than it does about Buddhism. I think the only way you can say that Buddhism is not a religion is if you have adopted the viewpoint of Buddhist modernism—perhaps especially the subset of Buddhist modernism that calls itself Secular Buddhism. As we discussed in chapter 7, this form of Buddhism prioritizes the philosophy, psychology, and neuroscience of meditation above all else. However, the overwhelming majority of Buddhists who live now and have lived in the past, both in Asia and elsewhere around the world, have not just focused on meditation. They have also believed in rebirth and merit-making; in the divinity and accomplishments of the buddhas and bodhisattvas;

in heavens and hells; in manifestation bodies and multiple worlds. And they have engaged in countless types of ritual practices that are associated with all of these beliefs.

This chapter is going to give you a whirlwind introduction to Buddhist rituals. In exploring this topic, we are going to be diving into matters that qualify as religious by any definition. Buddhist modernist books usually downplay or even ignore these aspects of Buddhism, because they don't square well with the modern materialist, scientific, or "spiritual not religious" worldviews. In contrast, because this book is Buddhish and not trying to convince you that Buddhism is correct about everything—and because I am not trying to talk you into adopting one or another type of Buddhism—I don't have to put a spin on Buddhism to make it more palatable to you or fit perfectly into your life. Instead, we can honestly explore Buddhist beliefs and the associated practices in a neutral and more objective way, without anyone feeling forced to either accept or reject them.

Let's start by accepting the simple fact that, far from being a marginal activity, ritual has been, hands-down, the most widespread aspect of Buddhism worldwide in all times and places. Thinking historically and globally, over the entire span of the existence of this tradition, only a small minority of Buddhists have done meditation, even fewer have gone forth, and a tiny fraction have been philosophers, but almost every Buddhist who has ever lived has practiced rituals of some sort or another.

1. MAGICAL ABILITIES

The basic premise behind most Buddhist rituals is that there are unseen forces out there in the universe that human beings can tap into and that can influence our lives. For example, all of the traditional schools of Buddhism say that serious meditation practice can result in acquiring magical or paranormal abilities (*siddhis*). Traditionally, these include powers that simply do not square with a modern scientific view of the world: the power to read minds, for example, or to fly, to appear in multiple locations, to grow or shrink, to remember past lives, to see everything in the universe, to shapeshift, to control the material world, and so forth and so on. Don't think for a moment that these might be tangential or fringe beliefs. You can check out the scriptures from literally every Buddhist tradition, and you will find that they are filled with examples of the Buddha, bodhisattvas, adept monks, and other notable people performing such magical feats. Because it is generally believed that the more advanced one becomes in spiritual practice, the greater these powers become, it is also common to represent perfected beings such as buddhas and bodhisattvas as completely omnipotent. In the *Instructions of Vimalakirti*, for example, they are said to be able to hold the entire universe within the palm of a hand. In the *Lotus Sutra*, to give another example, their bodies can emit blinding light from their pores that fills the multidimensional universe.

Traditional schools of Buddhism promise that you too can gain these kinds of supernormal abilities through practicing the Dharma. Practitioners often engage in special meditations, visualizations, and other rituals and exercises that are specifically intended to cultivate these magical powers. Masters of these arts go by different names in different Asian languages (*lersi, weikza, mahasiddha, tantrika, ngagpa*), and there are many culturally specific traditions and models of this kind of practice. Just Google some of those keywords, and you'll find yourself going down a rabbit hole into a radically different world of Buddhism than if you had limited yourself to reading about Secular Buddhism or mindfulness.

2. BLESSINGS

Buddhas, bodhisattvas, and other adept practitioners are thought to be able to share some of their acquired benefits with others through the act of blessing. A devotee might seek a blessing from a local monk, meditation teacher, or master ritualist by visiting them in person. Or they may reach out to a bodhisattva or buddha through prayer or by visiting a statue of that deity. Most likely, truly devout Buddhists would do all of the above on a regular basis. Seeking blessings could be done on a monthly, weekly, or often even daily basis. It might be intended to bring a bit of good luck more generally, or it may be geared toward a specific outcome—winning lottery numbers, a passing grade on an upcoming exam, prosperity for the family business, harmony in a marriage, boons of health and longevity, protection from disasters, and much, much more.

Those in a position to do so normally give blessings in response to or in exchange for ritual offerings. The specific objects that are offered can vary from tradition to tradition and place to place, but some common examples are flowers, incense, candles, fruit or other foods, money, and household goods. Normally, the devotee seeking a blessing engages in specific ritual actions when offering these objects, typically bowing and chanting or repeating certain ritual phrases. The person giving the blessing may then chant or enact other ritual actions in response. They may also give the devotee objects that contain their blessings, such as bracelets, amulets, water, food, and so forth, which could be worn, eaten, or stored for future use. While a blessing ritual can be big or small, and the details can vary, the basic logic is transactional: the seeker gives a gift symbolizing their respect and devotion, and receives a blessing in return.

From my own personal experience, I am most familiar with how this transaction plays out in Thailand. I have seen and participated in countless examples of blessing rituals. For example, I visited a famous *lersi* (wizard) in Bangkok, who I watched lay a ritual sword across the shoulders of a devotee in order to convey the blessing of physical protection, strength, and invincibility. I consulted a ritualist in a rural temple on the northern border who used a pen to write talismanic symbols on the crown of my head when my wife and I were seeking to have children. I witnessed a monk spray the facilities of a school where I worked in Chiang Mai with blessed water in order to create a zone of safety for the students and teachers. I saw a massage doctor in the Golden Triangle region hand out blessed amulets to his patients after conducting his treatments. And, every single morning in cities, towns, and villages across the country, I watched people line up in the streets to give offerings of food to monks as they passed through their neighborhoods.

The point is that, for Thai Buddhists, seeking blessings is completely commonplace, a normal part of everyday life. And that's not just true in Thailand. Although the details might differ based on sect and culture, it's similar all over the Buddhist world.

3. SPIRITS

One of the most common reasons to seek blessings in any Buddhist culture is to protect oneself from uncertainty. Unenlightened humans need divine protection, because misfortune, disease, disaster, calamity, or bad luck could befall us at any moment. Partially, these unfortunate outcomes might be due to karma, and many blessings are specifically intended to discharge your karmic debts. But it is also a common belief that we need specific ritual protections from the interference of malicious spirits.

Most Buddhists believe that a whole range of invisible spirit beings surround us: not just buddhas and bodhisattvas but also various higher-level gods and angelic beings; nature spirits associated with trees, mountains, streams, and other places; ancestral spirits, ghosts, and hell-beings associated with the dead; demons or evil spirits who want to cause harm to us; and beneficial spirits who want to help. Humans are constantly surrounded by and influenced by this whole panoply. Spirits can also enter our bodies and possess us if we are not careful, which can lead to mental and physical disease or pronounced bad luck. Because the outcome of our interactions with these beings is often uncertain, it pays to seek protective blessings as often as possible.

It is worthwhile to mention something comparatively unusual about Buddhism's approach to evil spirits. The approach to malicious beings in many religions seems to be to destroy them—to slay the dragons, to exorcize the demons, to defeat Satan, and so forth. Buddhist stories about overcoming evil, on the other hand, usually end with the conversion of the offending spirit to Buddhism. Once they are taught the error of their ways, the formerly evil entity is overcome by remorse at their previous behavior and becomes filled with compassion for suffering humans. They now become dedicated to protecting the Dharma and serving humans instead of harming them.

One prime example of the many such tales from around the Buddhist world is that of Padmasambhava, also known as Guru Rinpoche (Precious Master), who is the equivalent of the patron saint of Tibet. It is said that when he brought Buddhism to Tibet, Padmasambhava had to subdue various demons and evil spirits by converting them into protectors. This is one reason why the Tibetan pantheon has a number of evil-looking "wrathful" deities. These figures have demonic faces, but they are actually beneficial beings.

Not just in Tibet but in temples all around Asia, you'll find scary-looking *yaksa* spirits guarding the doorways, dragonlike *naga* spirits running down the staircases, and many other demons who preserve the Dharma and protect its followers. Once you start looking, you are likely to find converted evil spirits all over the place. Many of these spirits represent aspects of indigenous culture that were prevalent before the introduction of Buddhism and that were appropriated into the religion centuries ago as it spread across Asia. As the story of Padmasambhava suggests, rather than stamping out preexisting traditions, when Buddhism arrived in a new territory, it often found a way to incorporate local spirit practices into a Buddhist framework. These aspects of indigenous culture are what gives Buddhism a lot of its local flavor and diversity around the world.

In most Buddhist traditions, beneficial spirits are regularly given offerings in order to keep them happy and to garner their protection. In many parts of Southeast Asia, for example, families have "spirit houses," dollhouse-like structures outside their residences where they place food, water, incense, and flowers for spirits. These rituals are modest in their aims and quite simple in their execution, but spirit practices can also be elaborate, like the massive Liberation Rite of Water and Land that I attended at a temple in Taiwan. Designed to lift all spirit-beings out of suffering, this complex ritual was a multiday affair involving building a series of custom shrines, the burning of paper effigies, music and other performances, and massive feasts for a huge crowd of people.

In some Buddhist cultures, it is believed that your own body has spirit protectors that live inside you (Thai: *khwan*; Tibetan: *lha*) who can be given offerings or be honored in order to ensure your own safety, health, and well-being. In other traditions, demons or spirits are something akin to symbols or metaphorical representations of negative human emotions, and working with them is a way of helping to channel difficult feelings into being helpful for spiritual development. In any event, Buddhist tradition is filled with spirits everywhere you look—even inside your own body and mind.

4. RITUALS FOR SPIRITUAL PROGRESS

So far, I have been speaking about rituals that are intended to provide benefit to the devotee within the realm of everyday life—good luck, health, prosperity, and so forth. However, for many Buddhists, rituals can also be a central part of the spiritual path itself. For example, according to the teachings of the Pure Land School—a form of Buddhism that has been immensely popular in East Asia for centuries and is probably the most popular form of Mahayana in the world today in terms of numbers of adherents—it is virtually impossible to become Awakened in this lifetime by practicing meditation. The only hope we have is to call upon the all-powerful Amitabha Buddha (called Amida in Japanese and Amituo in Chinese). The primary practice in this school of Buddhism is to chant Amitabha's name over and over again. Those who wholeheartedly chant his name will find themselves reborn in the next life in his paradisiacal Pure Land, the Land of Bliss (Sukhavativyuha). They will be born into a lotus flower that opens up at Amitabha's feet. All their needs will be fulfilled, and Amitabha will teach them everything they need to know to become fully Awakened.

Another school of Buddhism, founded by the Japanese monk Nichiren (1222–1282), particularly emphasizes chanting the mantra "Nam Myoho Renge Kyo," or "Honor to the Sutra of the Lotus of Sublime Dharma." By invoking the name of the *Lotus Sutra*, this mantra is thought to invoke the blessings and protection of the Buddha and all of the bodhisattvas and other deities that are mentioned within that text. (While there are multiple temples and organizations that comprise the Nichiren school of Buddhism, one of the most visible today is Soka Gakkai International, the diverse mega-organization mentioned in chapter 10.)

While all traditional schools of Buddhism practice chanting scriptures or mantras, for both the Pure Land and Nichiren schools this practice is the core spiritual practice within their respective traditions. Rather than practicing meditation to become Awakened, they focus on calling upon powers beyond our own for salvation. This is often described as a form of "other-powered" practice, in contrast to the "self-powered" practice of meditation that is the norm within other forms of Buddhism.

5. NON-DUAL RITUALS

The idea that humans are incapable of realization on their own and need divine assistance or empowerment is, in the terms I introduced in chapter 9, a type of dualism. In fact, all of the rituals discussed thus far in this chapter posit a dualistic divide between us ordinary humans and the powerful "others" who can help us. So let's finish this chapter by adding some examples of rituals that symbolize or enact non-dualism, or the unification of dualities.

First, I'll mention the "deity yoga" rituals of Vajrayana Buddhism. (Here, the word "yoga" means "union" or "unification," not stretching.) Like all Vajrayana rituals, these practices are complex, multifaceted, and done differently by different lineages or teachers. One thing that all deity yoga practices have in common is that they center on the ability to visualize a Buddha or bodhisattva with all of their attributes and symbols. Once practitioners can call this image to mind in a stable way, they then perform various rituals and visualizations that meld the practitioner's own body and mind together with the deity's. Through this merger, the practitioner is thought to take on the identity, attributes, and powers of the deity in question. So now rather than praying to a deity to ask for its blessings, the blessings are fully integrated into the devotee's own being.

A different kind of union that is also a traditional part of Vajrayana Buddhism is ritualized sex. Sexuality plays a much smaller role in Buddhism as a whole than it does in some other Asian traditions, such as Tantric Hinduism, but you can find certain pockets of practitioners who have engaged in this type of practice. Usually, it involves visualization exercises rather than actual physical intercourse, although the latter practice is not unheard of. In general terms, the practice involves visualizing yourself having sexual relations with certain types of deities and exchanging energies with them (more on energies in chapter 15). Essentially, the idea is to harness the sexual energies of the human body and transform them into spiritual energies through an internal process of "alchemy" (rasayana). Similar to deity yoga, the symbolism here emphasizes the non-dual unification of the practitioner with the divine.

This sexual symbolism can also be seen in Tibetan sacred paintings and statues in which male-female pairs of buddhas or bodhisattvas (called yab-yum in Tibetan) are depicted with the female sitting in the male's lap, the two of them locked together in sexual intercourse. Again, this is a symbolic representation of non-dualism, in this case the unification of wisdom (female) and compassion or skillful means (male).

And that, my friends, brings our quick tour of Buddhist rituals to an end. Of course, Sariputra, the caricature of a conservative moralizing follower of an "Inferior Vehicle," would be scandalized that our final examples involve sex. But I think many modern Secular Buddhists would be equally scandalized by how rich and diverse Buddhist ritual traditions are. Many of them would write all of this off as superstitious nonsense that's totally missing the "real" point of Buddhism, which is to meditate.

My response to that is to ask, "Says who?" Who should determine what the real point of Buddhism is? Should it be you? I certainly don't think it should be me. I'd rather focus on describing what Buddhism actually is instead of telling you what I think it should be. Do all of these rituals we've talked about here square perfectly with the philosophical positions of impermanence, non-self, Nirvana, and emptiness? Maybe not. But who said that the doctrine and practice of *any* religion has to be totally consistent—never mind a tradition as old, complex, and multicultural as Buddhism?

15

WELL-BEING

As I am writing this chapter in summer of 2020, I am on the East Coast of the United States in a state of semi-isolation. The global outbreak of COVID-19 that occurred earlier this year has become a dire situation here. School buildings have been closed; communities have been on lockdown across the country; the death toll is mounting; the economy is crashing; and people everywhere are feeling panicked, anxious, or numb. Nearly six hundred thousand people have died from the virus so far, and this number is climbing every day.

Buddhists all around the world have been dealing with these months of global crisis in their own ways, and I have been following these different responses. If you were someone who thought all Buddhists were disengaged cave-dwelling meditators, all of this activity would be surprising to you. But, of course, by this point in the book, you know that it's not at all unexpected for Buddhists to be engaged in real-world issues in all kinds of different ways.

The fact is, whatever the historical era or geographic location, Buddhism has always been closely intertwined with both mental and physical well-being. This is my own particular area of academic research. Based on historical records I have studied from across ancient and medieval Asia, I can tell you that Buddhists have been thinking about the relationship between spiritual practice and health for as long as Buddhism has existed. Going back as far as the very earliest sanghas, Buddhist texts from India and elsewhere in Asia are filled with stories about how monks healed themselves through meditation or ritual practice, how they cared for each other when they were sick, and how they were familiar with the healing applications of all kinds of plants and medicinal substances.

A significant part of my academic research has focused on how the expansion of Buddhism around Asia in the premodern period was a catalyst for the spread of medical ideas and therapies. In places as diverse as Cambodia, Mongolia, Sri Lanka, Thailand, and Tibet, entire medical traditions developed that were based on Buddhism. Traditional Tibetan medicine, to give just one example, integrates herbal medicines, minor surgery, and pulse-reading with meditation, ritual, and other Buddhist practices into a holistic system. Called *Sowa Rigpa* (the Science of Healing), this tradition is said to have been founded by the Medicine Buddha himself. For centuries, it was developed and practiced within Buddhist monastic medical institutions.

This close relationship between Buddhism and medicine has continued to the present day, despite the almost complete transformation of medical science in the last 150 years. Today, many Buddhist institutions still are involved in promoting traditional Asian medicine, while others are closely involved with modern hospitals, biomedicine, and public health infrastructure. I discussed a prominent example, the Tzu Chi Foundation, in chapter 11. This Taiwanese organization has been visibly active in raising funds, donating medical supplies, and otherwise supporting efforts to help fight the current pandemic. Soka Gakkai International, which I mentioned in chapter 10, has been active in similar efforts. Many other smaller Buddhist organizations around the world have also been on the front lines, even if few have the clout and financial resources of these two massive organizations.

As a researcher specializing in the field of Buddhist medicine for several decades, I closely study the history as well as the contemporary practice of Buddhist and Buddhist-inspired healing globally. From this vantage point, I argue that Buddhism's single most important insight into health and well-being has been the idea that our mental state plays a major role in overall health. Of course, many other traditions have said that mental well-being directly leads to better health outcomes, but in Buddhism it's a central concept with a well-elaborated system of theory and practice.

Why is the mind so important to our health? In Buddhist terms, the mind and the body are not really two separate systems. Rather, they are thought of as different components of an interconnected whole. There's a term in Sanskrit, *namarupa*, which I've often seen translated as "bodymind," that captures this notion. From this integrative perspective, it doesn't make much sense to rigidly differentiate spiritual practice from healing, since religion and medicine both are collections of practices that operate on the same unified bodymind. Any techniques that can bring relief, solace, happiness, or peace to the mind automatically will have beneficial effects on the body as well, and vice versa.

Buddhism offers unique health interventions that flow from this idea of a unified bodymind. For example, one approach that both ancient texts and contemporary teachers talk a lot about is reflecting on the emptiness of illness. It might be difficult to remember this in these times of crisis and panic, but Buddhist philosophy would say that the word "coronavirus" is just as empty as any other concept. From the perspective of the ultimate truth, we can deconstruct this particular form into its constituent components. We can see that the virus is just a collection of molecules, atoms, or quantum particles. If your body is invaded by the virus, it's just particles over here joining up with some other particles over there, and this doesn't ultimately matter from the perspective of emptiness. The universe continues on, vast and perfect just "as it is."

This kind of perspective can seem coldhearted, but remember from our discussion in chapter 10 that no one is suggesting we use emptiness to paper over the suffering of others. Emptiness alone is a broken one-wheeled cart. Nevertheless, when we ourselves get sick, reflecting on the impersonal and non-self nature of this process could perhaps give us some relief from the anxiety of dwelling on questions such as "Why me?" that only exacerbate our duhkha.

In addition to offering reflections on the emptiness of illness, Buddhist teachers and authors have for many centuries been advocating meditation as a means of promoting health. As I mentioned in chapter 8, the most prevalent example of this approach today is the mindfulness-based stress reduction protocol. Since the invention of MBSR in 1979, tens of thousands of research papers have been published on mindfulness and other meditations (many of which are readily accessible on the PubMed.gov database). On the whole, this research has shown that meditation is able to positively impact health and well-being in measurable ways. The press has seized on these results, presenting meditation as if it were a panacea for just about any ailment whatsoever. Scientists themselves have been more reserved in their enthusiasm, but now, after several decades of research, they are confident that meditation has an important role to play in the treatment of anxiety, depression, chronic pain, and some other conditions. Scientific research has also demonstrated how meditation changes the brain, hormones, and other biological systems in ways that are conducive to health.

Given all of these facts, it's not surprising to see that many Buddhist leaders and communities around the world are responding to the current pandemic by encouraging people to meditate. And I have recently interviewed many Buddhists who say that their meditation practice has helped them to manage the stress, anxiety, and uncertainty of the current situation.

At the same time, Buddhist leaders have been advocating that people be generous and patient with each other and that we use the crisis as an opportunity to practice having gentler minds, kinder hearts, and a lot more self-compassion. Scientific research on compassion-based practices (such as the one I discussed in chapter 13) has begun to validate these as health interventions as well (also available on PubMed.gov). It now seems clear that all of these recommendations are not just religious platitudes but indeed also sound health advice.

Focusing on reducing stress and developing positive states of mind are nearly universal Buddhist approaches advocated by virtually all Buddhist communities. Other practices are specific to particular groups. For example, many Buddhists feel that there are ways to intervene more directly in the pandemic using rituals. People might engage in prayer, chanting, or offerings to various buddhas or bodhisattvas to gain protection from the virus or to ensure that they recover quickly if they come down with the illness. The Dalai Lama and other major leaders with global followings have told Buddhists to engage in this kind of ritual. Whereas the specific deity might be different from place to place or case to case, the Medicine Buddha, Avalokitesvara, and Tara are particularly popular choices among Mahayanists. Many Buddhists are stepping up their offerings to these beings in order to gain their blessings, and many temples are consequently running a full calendar of these ritual events remotely during the pandemic via Zoom, YouTube, Facebook, and other online platforms.

If you read the previous chapter, you also won't be surprised to learn that a whole range of magically charged talismans, amulets, and other objects are also being used for protection against COVID-19. For example, Buddhist temples in Thailand are distributing masks with protective talismans printed on them. In Sri Lanka, blessed water has been sprayed onto entire villages from helicopters overhead in an effort to protect whole communities. In Japan, monks have tweeted photos of Vairocana Buddha meant to bless anyone who lays eyes on him. As we discussed at some length in the previous chapter, such practices are not anomalous; they are all well within the scope of normal Buddhist practice.

Many of these Buddhist responses to the pandemic are based on the idea that the bodymind is permeated with a "subtle energy," a life force that is constantly flowing, keeping everything moving, growing, changing, and becoming. In East Asian forms of Buddhism, this energy is normally talked about using the Chinese term *qi* or the Japanese equivalent *ki* (pronounced "chee" and "kee" respectively). One of the best ways to stay healthy, according to this view, is to ensure that the flow of energy is strong and unhindered by any blockages due to unhealthy mental habits or physical behaviors. Traditionally, East Asian Buddhists have thought that the flow of qi or ki can be facilitated and blockages corrected using acupuncture, breathing exercises, movement techniques, certain diets, herbs, and a range of other practices. In the age of COVID-19, all of these techniques have taken on new urgency for practitioners, both in Asia and around the world.

In Vajrayana Buddhism, these bodymind energies are spoken of as "winds." Called *rlung* (pronounced "loong") in Tibetan, these winds function much like qi or ki in East Asian traditions. Vajrayana texts describe a system of channels throughout the body along which rlung energy flows. However, Vajrayana departs from the East Asian model by adding the notion of the chakras. The Sanskrit word (properly transliterated *cakra*) simply means "wheel," and the chakras are akin to whirling wheels of energy in the body.

Vajrayana Buddhism shares its model of winds, channels, and chakras with some other Tantric traditions that originated in India, such as Hindu systems of yoga. In a nutshell, the idea in most of these systems is that, while the subtle winds flow everywhere throughout the body, there are three main channels that run up the midline of the body from the genitals to the crown of the head. Located along that central axis, there are a number of chakras (exactly how many differs from tradition to tradition), which are locations where certain energies originate and are stored, manipulated, or cultivated. Practitioners work with mantras, visualizations, breath work, and physical yoga postures to develop control over these energies and move them intentionally through the system of channels and chakras.

In Vajrayana Buddhism, particularly as practiced in Tibet, there are a number of different traditions and teachings about how to do this (see, for example, Yantra Yoga). The ultimate goal is always to be able to use these subtle winds to facilitate spiritual development. That being said, they say that you can use these same techniques to promote good health, to cure disease, and to extend your lifetime longer than it normally would be. That, of course, is quite relevant when it comes to the coronavirus pandemic, and right now there are many leading Tibetan Buddhists who are advocating these types of practices to help people prevent or cure COVID-19.

I myself have never studied any of these Tibetan practices. However, I did study a similar system while I was living in Thailand. In addition to spending time at meditation centers and at monasteries, I was an avid student of traditional Thai medicine for about four years. This form of healing is heavily influenced by Buddhism, and it integrates both meditation and Buddhist ritual into its core practices. Interestingly, even though Thai Buddhism is not a form of Vajrayana, traditional medicine in Thailand incorporates many of the ideas about subtle winds (in Thai called *lom*) I just described.

My exposure to these ideas came mostly when I was learning a healing practice called *nuad boran*. This term is most often translated as "Thai massage," but it's really a therapy that combines massage, chiropractic work, and yoga therapy in order to affect the flows of subtle winds in the body. The idea in the school where I learned the technique was to press and move the patient's body in synch with their breathing in order to charge up, clear, or reset their entire energetic system. Whereas Vajrayana frames working with the subtle winds as a technique that leads to quicker Awakening, my experience in Thailand involved an entirely medical application of the same models.

How do these ideas sound to you? Before I was exposed to this kind of practice in Thailand, I would have said that the notion of bodymind energy was a far-out kind of spiritual fantasy. But through a combination of practicing Thai massage and the kind of meditation I introduced in chapter 8 that is focused on mindfulness of body sensations, I eventually became quite attuned to how my body feels on the inside. As a result, I realized that talk about subtle energies or winds is at its core an elaborate cluster of metaphors that clearly describes—and tunes you in to—how the sensations in your body change in response to your mind. I don't think there's necessarily anything mystical or supernatural going on here. Rather, I see it as a culturally specific way of describing a common everyday experience that all human beings share—and that any of us can notice if we pay attention.

You can begin to feel what Buddhists refer to as bodymind energies if you start paying attention to what happens internally when you have a strong emotion. Take anxiety, for example. How do you know you're anxious? What exactly does it feel like? In my own experience, the initial provocation that causes anxiety to arise is a thought. That thought triggers a clenching in a specific location deep in my abdomen. Then a wave of jittery or fluttering body sensations rises from that location vertically toward my heart. This feeling can cause my heart rate to increase and my breathing to get faster. I then usually experience a cold tingling sensation that rises from my chest up to my shoulders, neck, and head, which then floods the rest of my body. Do you feel something similar in your body when you experience anxiety? Next time, take a look and see.

With a bit of practice and close attention, you can also begin to understand what people mean when they speak of controlling or manipulating these responses. Again, speaking from personal experience, I have learned that once that anxious feeling starts up in my body, it can start my mind off on a spiral of anxious thoughts. This activity in turn can trigger more clenching in my gut, which results in a cascade of sensations that grows more and more intense until it seems to take over my whole bodymind. But I have also learned that I can intervene in this process. As soon as I notice anxiety in my body, I can take a deep breath and just observe the tension or tingling at that spot with a neutral mindset. Sometimes it takes a few breaths, but if I've got enough concentration and am able to relax into the sensations without reacting to them, I can often calm my whole system down quickly.

Is your experience of anxiety the same as or different from mine? Maybe you would use different words than I have, but can you relate to the feelings I'm describing? Could you also see how someone else may choose to describe these same experiences in terms of an agitated wind that moves along specific channels and that can start or get stuck in certain spinning wheels located in their torso?

Personally, I don't think that language is bizarre or even off-base. Of course, if it's unhelpful for you to think in terms of these metaphors, then feel free to use others. Or just focus on examining the experience without getting hung up on the words. I think the main point Buddhism is trying to get across is that it's helpful for your health to improve your interoception, your attention to what's going on inside your body. When you pay more attention to what's going on inside, you can see how the mind triggers negative reactions in the body and the body responds to the mind. Once you can observe this process in real time, you can learn ways to intervene in order to bring yourself a bit of relief.

Dramatic feelings like anxiety are a good place to start, but as you learn to notice the fluctuations of your bodymind, you can cultivate more and more subtle levels of interoception. Improved awareness of how your body feels on an ongoing basis might help you to better regulate your sleep, your diet, your exercise, and other facets of your life in order to optimize your mental and physical well-being. Instead of allowing yourself to become controlled by unconscious habits, you might better tune into the natural rhythms inherent to your body. Maybe you could even sense when something is going awry right from the beginning and intuitively know how to intervene most effectively before any major symptoms appear.

Eventually, the practice gets even more subtle than that. If you continue to explore your energies in ever more sensitive ways, you can find yourself experiencing a deep healing of the entire bodymind. Many Buddhists would say that taking this kind of work seriously can ultimately result in Awakening. Others prefer to focus on the concrete benefits for mental and physical well-being. I'll leave it up to you to decide whether to call this religion or medicine, but I think you'll agree that the line between them in this case is quite blurry.

It may come as no surprise that a common metaphor used throughout the Buddhist traditions is that Buddha is the Great Doctor. They say that he has diagnosed humanity's ultimate ailment as a severe case of duhkha and that he has given us a prescription in the form of the Dharma. Many Buddhists worldwide have been turning to this range of teachings to ensure their well-being in these uncertain times. Trusting in the Dharma has been a source of great comfort in the current pandemic, as it has been in times of epidemics and other health crises throughout history.

16

ZEN

Zen is a challenging topic to discuss. Partially, this is because inscrutability is an intentional feature of the tradition. As we have already mentioned briefly in chapter 9, paradox lies at its very core. Whether it's the Buddha-nature hidden in plain sight or koans such as the "sound of one hand clapping," Zen is not something that one can quickly grok from a couple of paragraphs. It's something you have to soak in for a while, slowly relaxing into it and letting it sink into you.

Zen, you might remember from chapter 7, is the Japanese pronunciation of the Chinese word *chan*, which generically means "meditation" (or more technically "meditative absorption"). The word is used to refer to a trend in Buddhist practice that first emerged in China in the sixth and seventh centuries CE. The story Zen tells about itself is that it is a method of pointing directly to one's Buddha-nature that was handed down from the time of the Buddha as a separate transmission outside Buddhist scriptural tradition.

The legendary Indian monk Bodhidharma (known in Japanese as Daruma) is said to have brought the Zen tradition to China in the fifth century. The myth of Bodhidharma says that he went into deep meditation inside a cave, facing the blank cavern wall, for a period of nine years. He is also said to have cut off his eyelids to prevent sleep, and when his eyelids fell to the ground, they sprouted into the first tea plant. This, they say, is how East Asia's favorite stimulant came to be closely associated with Buddhism.

In any event, when Zen spread to Japan in the twelfth century, this school grew into a distinctive and unique tradition. There are two highly influential branches of Japanese Zen: Soto and Rinzai. Both strongly emphasize seated meditation, or *zazen*. However, they have their doctrinal and practical differences, with Soto noted for its emphasis on the formless meditation of "just sitting" (see chapter 9) and Rinzai noted for its emphasis on koans (also in chapter 9).

While all forms of Buddhism are influenced by the cultures and times in which they are practiced, Zen, more than most, is a distinctively East Asian form of Buddhism. In addition to its strong emphasis on meditation, Zen draws on a number of native Chinese influences that shaped it intellectually, culturally, and aesthetically. One major source of inspiration is the non-dual Chinese philosophy of Daoism, from which it borrowed some key concepts and terminology. ("Daoism," also spelled "Taoism," is just as multifaceted a term as "Buddhism," referring to many diverse and often contradictory schools of thought and practice from China. But let's set that aside for another book.)

Also influenced by Daoism is Zen's deep appreciation of the natural world. In this regard, Zen seems to move in the opposite direction of many other types of Buddhism, which often can seem quite disconnected from nature. In my own experience learning meditation in the Theravada tradition, for example, I was taught that if my mind wandered away from the breath or body sensations for any reason, including even pleasant aspects of nature, it was a distraction. If the goal is to remain constantly, single-mindedly focused on a meditation object, then a chirping bird outside the meditation hall can never be anything more than a source of interference. Several Theravada meditation centers I frequented even had isolation cells, tiny pitch-black soundproofed rooms, where I would spend ten days in almost total sensory deprivation in order to avoid such disruptions and concentrate more deeply. When we left our cells to go to the bathroom or eat, practitioners always kept our eyes fixed on our feet and our attention glued to the meditation object.

By contrast, in the Zen practice of "just sitting," one keeps one's attention wide open, choicelessly accepting anything that comes into one's awareness, chirping birds and all. Far from tuning them out, it seems that sounds, sights, and other perceptions become heightened by this kind of practice. You start to perceive things more crisply, and everything can seem more beautiful than ever. This enhanced perception may be one reason that Zen masters have frequently celebrated the natural world and have lovingly dwelt on small details in the environment.

Since the medieval period, nature has been one of the most common themes in cultural expressions associated with Zen, most notably in poetry and landscape painting. These art forms typically minimize the presence of humans, preferring to represent intimate scenes from the natural world that are untouched by the "artificiality" of human affairs. Particularly influential in crafting Zen's connection with nature was Eihei Dogen (1200–1253), the founder of the Soto school, who introduced the practice of just sitting to Japan and who was one of the most celebrated Zen masters of all time. In his *Mountains and Waters Sutra* (*Sansui Kyo*), Dogen poetically characterizes nature as a scripture that can be understood as an expression of Buddha-nature and read as the very essence of the Buddha's teachings.

Understanding this connection between Zen and nature helps us to appreciate why this haiku by Matsuo Basho (1644–1694) is considered one of the greatest pieces of Japanese literature ever:

An old pond.
A frog jumps.
The sound of water.

Haiku are, as you probably know, three lines long, with five syllables in the first line, seven in the second line, and five in the third. Under these extremely limited constraints, Basho's poem transports us to the banks of a silent pond, perhaps far out in the woods. In the stillness of this scene, a frog's sudden motion catches our eye, and a single splash of water breaks the silence. The moment is fleeting, reflective of both the quiet stillness and the spontaneous activity of the natural world. It reminds us to watch and listen, to be fully present to our moment-to-moment experience.

The resonance between Zen, nature, and poetry continues to flourish in the present day. The American poet and early Western adopter of Zen, Gary Snyder (b. 1930), even explicitly connected the Zen appreciation for nature with ecological activism. His famous 1969 poem "Smokey the Bear Sutra" was a call to action that played a role in launching the modern environmental movement. In fact, there are a lot of Buddhist concepts that lend themselves to environmental awareness, such as interdependence and nonviolence, and there are many contemporary Buddhists who are active in this area of skillful means.

The high point of Zen aesthetics came, arguably, a century after Dogen's death, in the Muromachi period (1338–1573). During this time, not only poetry and painting but also Japanese architecture, ceramics, and many other arts and aspects of culture were heavily influenced by Zen's sensitivity toward the natural world. This period spawned an aesthetic the Japanese call *wabi-sabi*. While it is a hard phrase to translate literally, wabi-sabi has been described as the material representation or aesthetic expression of Zen philosophy. Wabi-sabi emphasizes themes from nature and a rustic simplicity unadorned or undisturbed by humans. It also involves an appreciation for imperfections, an orientation toward the impermanence of the natural world, and a certain austerity created by an emphasis on empty space.

Can you picture a Japanese Zen temple in your mind? What about a Japanese teahouse? Wabi-sabi is the reason that these structures look the way they do. They are intentionally simple, made mostly of bare wood or other natural materials, with lots of empty space inside. There might be a single black and white scroll against one wall or a sprig of flower in a simple vase for ornamentation. The simple sensibility reflected in such architecture and interior design contrasts markedly with the loud and colorful Buddhist aesthetic from virtually every other part of Asia. If you don't know what I'm talking about, just Google an image of a Japanese Zen temple and compare it with an image of a Buddhist temple from Taiwan, Tibet, Cambodia, or anywhere else. What a difference!

Wabi-sabi also plays a role in Zen calligraphy and brush painting. These art forms characteristically emphasize themes from nature. A painting might consist simply of a few flowers against a blank background. Compare this subtle, impressionistic, and sparse aesthetic to the dramatic, colorful, and garish vibe of a Tibetan, Mongolian, or Nepalese *thangka* painting. (Again, just spend a little bit of time Googling if you don't know what I mean by these terms.)

Another aspect that separates Zen brushwork from other forms of Buddhist art is its spontaneity. I've attended a Zen calligraphy exhibition before, and it was really something to see. The artist stood before a blank piece of paper, brush and ink at the ready. As the crowd waited silently, she went into a meditative state, settling her mind into emptiness. Then, at a seemingly random moment, she sprang into action, picking up the brush, dipping it into the ink, and executing a circle (called an *enso* in Japanese) all in one stroke. If I had blinked, I might have missed it: it was completed in the time it took for her to exhale a single breath.

This kind of performance is intimately related to the interplay between emptiness and form, which is central to Zen. The idea is that the form painted on the paper came out of the emptiness of the artist's meditation. When forms spontaneously arise from the place of emptiness, they are perfect expressions of that very moment. Whatever they look like—even if there are what might be perceived of as flaws, such as the brush running out of ink in a particular part of the stroke or a splat of ink falling on the paper unexpectedly—they are perfect just as they are, because they are manifestations of the artist's Buddha-nature in that moment.

There are many other Japanese cultural activities that are influenced by the interplay between emptiness and form. In Zen-style archery (*kyudo*), for example, archers empty their minds before releasing an arrow, without aiming at the target in the conventional sense of the word. The tea ceremony (*chado*) is another example: preparing a simple cup of tea becomes a highly ritualized event.

You'll notice the suffix *-do* (pronounced something like the English word "doe") on the end of both *kyudo* and *chado*, as well as on the word for calligraphy, *shodo*, the word for flower arrangement, *kado*, and on the words for many other traditional Japanese arts. On its own, *do* means "path" or "way." When you add *do* to an activity in Japanese, you are implying that it is no longer a conventional activity but an intentional practice. You're no longer just doing calligraphy or shooting arrows or arranging flowers or drinking tea. Rather, you have elevated these activities to rituals with great significance. It's now a matter of form arising spontaneously out of emptiness, an expression of your Buddha-nature, an enactment of the non-dual union of ultimate truth and conventional truth.

To become a *do*, a practice requires years—decades, in fact—of training and a very high level of expertise. The Zen emphasis on naturalness does not mean that actions are unplanned—the whole idea is that it takes intricate focus and exactitude to execute a simple spontaneous action. With the right attention to detail and the right mindset, however, anything at all can be a *do*. At least that's my interpretation. If you remain grounded in emptiness, allow the actions to spontaneously occur, and are unattached to the outcomes, your whole life can be a *do*. Every mundane action can be transmuted into an expression of your Buddha-nature. What would it be like to live life from that place?

Cooking, plating a meal, and even washing dishes can be a *do*. If you don't believe me, watch the Korean Zen nun Jeong Kwan, who is featured on season 3, episode 1 of the Netflix show *Chef's Table*. I haven't eaten food prepared by Jeong Kwan herself, but I have spent several months in Korea and have eaten many meals at Korean temples.

The attention to the details of every aspect of the meal is impressive, and the chefs' skill is obvious. Rather than one dish, you are served ten or a dozen small plates, each one beautifully presented as an individual dish and perfectly balanced in relation to the others to contribute to the whole meal. Rather than being overpowered with spices or added flavors, each individual ingredient is given the opportunity to take the stage and shine in its own right, as if it were being given the space to express its own Buddha-nature, just as it should be. Planning, preparing, and serving this kind of meal is a high-level spiritual activity. As for me, though, I prefer to practice the *do* of eating!

I'm kidding, but Zen's proclivity for turning ordinary aspects of life into ritualized activities grounded in emptiness is sometimes not a joking matter. There's a dark side to this perspective that's well worth mentioning. You might have heard that historically Zen was adopted by the samurai warrior class that ruled over Japan for centuries and that it was influential in governing samurai behavior, mental discipline, and values. These connections between Zen and martial culture came to be emphasized in the late nineteenth and early twentieth centuries, and many Japanese people in that era became very excited about *bushido*—the "*do* of the warrior."

Reinterpreted in this context, Zen ideas were swept up in the nationalism and warmongering that were running rampant in Japan leading up to World War II. The art of war was characterized as a sacred duty and a spiritual path. Zen practices were modified for use in military training. Major Buddhist leaders supported the war effort, conducted fundraising activities for the purchase of military supplies, and gave spiritual justification for the suicide missions of kamikaze pilots. Zen temples were complicit in this process, establishing branch temples in territories conquered by Japan, such as Korea and Taiwan, where they served the interests of the colonial authorities.

While some major Zen organizations in Japan have since apologized for their actions during the war years, some of the broader implications of the linkage between Buddhism and warfare are still with us. During the Iraq War, the US military used meditation to increase soldiers' concentration, marksmanship, and resilience in preparation for battle. The design of this program, called Warrior Mind Training, specifically drew upon the image of the Japanese samurai as the noble warrior-meditator. A Norwegian right-wing terrorist who executed seventy-seven people in 2011 also claimed to have drawn inspiration from the bushido code of the samurai, specifically saying he used it to desensitize himself in preparation for the killings.

My students often are surprised to learn that Buddhists have not always been completely nonviolent and that Buddhist ideas have been used to propagate war or even to produce cold-blooded murderous terrorists. Perhaps you are surprised as well. But let's face it, Buddhism is not some kind of special case that's categorically different from all other religions or ideologies. Like all others, it has been and likely will continue to be adapted to serve the worst aspects of human nature as well as the best.

In my opinion, forms of Buddhism that overly emphasize the emptiness side of the middle way equation are in particular danger of being co-opted in this way. As we discussed in chapter 10, if you adopt an emptiness-only perspective, you might be tempted to argue that nothing in this world is ultimately real, so nothing you do ultimately matters. The vast majority of Buddhists, however, would be appalled at this kind of nihilism and would point out that only a deep and thorough misunderstanding of the Dharma could lead you to use the Buddha's teachings as a tool to increase your capacity to kill.

17

BUDDHIST

I started out this book by saying that I don't identify as Buddhist. But that hasn't always been true. I'd say my relationship with Buddhism has been complicated. As I've described, when I first engaged in Buddhist practice in a serious way in my early twenties, I threw myself into meditation. If you'd asked me about religion during those five years, I would have told you confidently that I was Theravada Buddhist. I lived for most of that time in Thailand, practiced two hours of meditation a day, spent lots of time at retreats and in monasteries, and yearned to become Awakened. I also spent a lot of time learning about the cultural side of Buddhism, visiting temples and sacred sites, as well as studying the Thai healing practices I mentioned in chapter 15.

However, after some years of intensive practice, I became increasingly burned-out by my goal-oriented approach. The final straw came when I spent the summer on retreat at a monastery in rural Thailand. As I talked about in chapter 13, a monk recommended I do reflections on compassion as a kind of antidote to my previous goal-oriented style. I'm not sure what his intention was, but for me this new practice elicited another profound shift. My experience that summer made my heart open up. I learned that, for me, if Awakening was going to happen at all, it was going to have to unfold while I was an active participant in the world, not isolated from it.

Upon leaving the monastery in 2001, I moved to the United States, entered graduate school, got married, and started a family. Over the next few years, I became increasingly involved in the academic study of Buddhism. I actively tried to practice wisdom and compassion within my life, but I no longer practiced meditation in any serious way. I did some ethnographic work in Buddhist temples in Asia and the United States, but I never joined a Buddhist community or group. Over time, I identified less and less as Buddhist. Much later, in my forties, long after I had abandoned the practice of meditation and the goal of Awakening, I experienced a series of spontaneous non-dual spiritual insights. Perhaps ironically, these happened completely outside of a Buddhist context, so I won't be discussing them here.

Now I like to joke that I'm Buddhish. Buddhism has continued to speak to me. I think many of its ideas are interesting, its stories are inspirational, and the richness and diversity of Buddhist cultures are endlessly fascinating. Recently, I am finding myself meditating again in a style similar to just sitting. At the same time, I also have become much more aware of Buddhism's blind spots, shortcomings, and even its dangers. I have lost any kind of romanticized or idealized view of the tradition and any desire to protect it from scrutiny or criticism.

Does it matter to you if your tour guide is Buddhist or not? I can tell you that one of the most common questions I get from students in my religious studies classes is "Are you Buddhist?" I can always tell that they're trying to size me up when they ask it. I've noticed that they really want a definitive yes or no answer. If I tell them that I'm Buddhish, that is not a satisfying answer. They really don't like blurry categories.

Actually, though, I don't think the categories are so clear-cut even when people do clearly identify themselves as Buddhist. What exactly does someone mean when they say, "I'm Buddhist"? In my experience, it can mean radically different things to different people. Some people these days might call themselves Buddhist when all they really mean is that they like to read books by Pema Chodron, Bhante Gunaratana, or other popular Buddhist authors. These people are sometimes disparagingly called "nightstand" Buddhists, because the books on their nightstands are their only connection with Buddhism. Some such people may be genuinely interested in what Buddhism has to offer and may feel some resonance with Buddhist notions such as meditation and compassion. If they want to label themselves Buddhist, I personally don't think there's anything wrong with that. As the great eighth-century Indian Buddhist philosopher Santideva put it, the desire to Awaken (*bodhicitta*) starts with a small thought.

But I do recommend thinking clearly about your motivations before you adopt the label Buddhist. In particular: Are you calling yourself that because you genuinely feel connected to the tradition or simply because you think it's cool to be Buddhist? In my opinion, if you're going to call yourself Buddhist, you should commit to educating yourself about the tradition.

Scholars have a concept, Orientalism, which refers to non-Asians projecting positive stereotypes onto Asian people or things. These positive stereotypes often lead non-Asians to culturally appropriate Asian objects and traditions they know next to nothing about. For example, someone who knows very little about Buddhism might place a Buddha statue in their home, wear Buddhist prayer beads, or tattoo themselves with Buddhist symbols because they want to give the outward appearance of being spiritual.

From what I can tell, Buddhists are split on this kind of cultural appropriation. Most of them see the tradition as universal and suitable for people of any culture or ethnicity. The Buddha himself is said to have told his disciples to fan out across the land and teach the Dharma in all locales and languages. Many Asian Buddhists I know personally have expressed the idea that forms of nightstand Buddhism or cultural appropriation are beneficial in the end, because they spread the word about Buddhism, even if in a superficial way. That is to say, they see these as forms of skillful means that might eventually draw people toward studying the Dharma.

But, I also know Asian American Buddhists who feel that Western Buddhism has been "whitewashed." When the popular media feature meditation, they tend to use photos of white people, and they frequently fail to mention the Asian cultural background behind Buddhist practice. Prominent bloggers and other critics have complained about this state of affairs, lamenting the erasure or devaluation of the many contributions Asian Americans have made to American Buddhism since they arrived in the United States in the middle of the nineteenth century.

Whatever their race or cultural background, all of the Buddhists I know draw the line at the most egregious types of Orientalism and appropriation, such as when companies capitalize on Buddhism's positive stereotypes to sell completely unrelated products. Across the Western world, once you start looking, you will find tea, bath salts, popcorn, beer, and all kinds of other commodities branded as "Buddha this" or "Zen that." Frequently, a picture of the Buddha or some other similar imagery is featured on the packaging as well, usually done in a caricatured and stereotyped way. What exactly is Buddhist about that bag of popcorn? Nothing. It's a marketing ploy to make you feel as if the product is somehow all-natural or relaxing. Next time you encounter one of these products on the shelf, just imagine how a Buddhist might feel about this particular use of their sacred imagery. Do you think they would feel flattered or belittled?

While we're on the subject, I want to share with you the worst example of cultural appropriation of a sacred image ever: the swastika. The swastika is a symbol that was used all over ancient Eurasia as a sign of good luck and auspiciousness (the word means "conducive to well-being" in Sanskrit). It continues to be a prevalent symbol in Buddhism, and you can see swastikas adorning temples, decorating sacred objects, and even emblazoned on the chest of Buddhist statues all over Asia. Even after Hitler used the symbol in his Nazi emblem, it was never associated with Nazism or Aryan ideology in Buddhist cultures. As a result, it never lost its positive connotations. (I can't describe the look I got from my students the time I forgot to mention the history of swastikas before beginning my Intro to Buddhism slideshow!)

Anyway, let's get back to our discussion about Buddhist identity. Even among serious practitioners, what it means to be Buddhist is not clear-cut. For a Western practitioner, for example, calling themselves Buddhist might mean that they have a serious meditation practice and are dedicating a significant amount of their life to striving for Awakening. But it's very possible that they have never been to a temple, never met a member of the sangha, and never bowed in front of a Buddha statue.

Someone who was born into an Asian Buddhist household could have a very different relationship with the term "Buddhist." For them, Buddhism might revolve around family, heritage, and cultural connection. These individuals might have grown up attending temple services with their parents and grandparents. They may have met plenty of monastics and may know all the rituals by heart. It's possible that they are serious meditators, since meditation is a Buddhist practice that is popular all over the world. But it's also quite possible that they never have done any meditation at all. It's even conceivable that they're a bit bored by or dismissive of the idea of Awakening or that they associate Buddhist teachings with the conservative moralizing of their elders. Yet, if such a person chooses to call themselves Buddhist, they have every right to do so, don't they?

My point is that just because someone claims a Buddhist identity doesn't necessarily tell you anything about their practice, their beliefs, or their engagement with any other specific facet of Buddhism. That being said, these different meanings of the term "Buddhist" can become contentious when one group of practitioners starts to argue that only people who practice like they do are "real" Buddhists. Someone who is zealous about their own particular definition, for example, might write off someone else as a fraudulent Buddhist if they don't do meditation or if they've never gone through the formal ritual of "taking refuge" (see next chapter), or some other criteria.

Conflicts like this can become more complex and even nasty if they get mixed together with other types of identity politics. You might be aware, for example, that in Myanmar, where about 90 percent of the population is Buddhist, conflicts between Buddhists and non-Buddhists are a major political and human rights issue. Beginning in 2016, the Rohingya people, a Muslim ethnic group in the western part of the country, were targeted and driven out of the country by the Myanmar government. About seven hundred thousand people were displaced, and once they were forced out, local Buddhist residents seized their land. In the process, tens of thousands of Rohingya were killed. International observers have since 2016 been documenting a staggering number of murders, rapes, arsons, and other atrocities against the Rohingya, committed both by the Myanmar military and by local Buddhist civilians. The United Nations has labelled these events ethnic cleansing and genocide.

"Wait," you say. "*Buddhists* committed those violent crimes against humanity?" Um, yeah. If that strikes you as impossible, you've still got some overly romanticized ideas about Buddhism of which I need to disabuse you. Time to wake up and smell that cup of coffee we brewed back in chapter 9! In this particular case, the fact that the Rohingya aren't Buddhist was *the* major reason why the Buddhist majority thought they did not belong in the country. Not only that, but among the chief instigators of the uprising were several influential Buddhist monks, whose inflammatory speeches were directly responsible for inciting the violence.

While what has happened in Myanmar is an example of how the mix of Buddhist identity and ethnic identity can go very, very wrong, let's follow up with an example of how Buddhist identity has been used as a catalyst for positive social change. Bhimrao Ramji Ambedkar (1891–1956) was a towering figure in Indian history: an intellectual who was instrumental in the Indian independence movement and independent India's first Minister of Law and Justice. In 1956, just before his death, Ambedkar converted to Buddhism and launched a new form of Buddhism he called Navayana (the New Vehicle). This movement began with the mass conversion to Buddhism of hundreds of thousands of Dalits (members of the so-called untouchable caste in Hinduism). Converting to Navayana specifically removed the Hindu converts' low caste status and was intended as a way to overcome the prejudice and social ostracism experienced by Dalits in Hindu society.

Ambedkar's New Vehicle involved the retooling of Buddhism, a complete reinterpretation of many of the central tenets of the tradition to optimize them for a social justice movement. Most social movements involving humanistic Buddhism and engaged Buddhism before and since have arisen within the context of traditional—usually Mahayana—Buddhism. As a result of his more revolutionary actions, Ambedkar received plenty of criticism from mainstream Buddhists, who claimed he had changed the essence of the Dharma. Truth be told, however, Navayana was neither the first nor the last new religious movement that used Buddhist ideas in the promotion of a brand-new vision of a utopian society.

Ambedkarites call themselves Buddhists, but are they—or the followers of other new hybrid forms of Buddhism—"real" Buddhists? Are those genocidal monks in Myanmar "real" Buddhists? Are people who attend temple but don't meditate "real" Buddhists? Are serious meditators who have never done the ritual to convert to Buddhism "real" Buddhists? Are nightstand Buddhists "real" Buddhists? Where do we draw the lines? And whose criteria do we use to draw them? I, for one, don't believe I have any business evaluating people's beliefs and practices in order to define who is a "real" Buddhist and who is not. And I'm not interested in defending Buddhism against "fake Buddhists." Being Buddhish rather than Buddhist, I don't feel a need to police the boundary of Buddhism. Do you?

In my book, anyone who calls themselves Buddhist is a type of Buddhist. On this point, I'd rather be descriptive than prescriptive. Being prescriptive means trying to mandate to other people how they should see an issue. For example, when I was talking about cultural appropriation of Buddhist imagery, I was being prescriptive, because I was trying to convince you that using Buddhist sacred images to sell products is disrespectful. However, this chapter as a whole focuses on a descriptive discussion of Buddhist identity. That is to say, providing a neutral description of how different people have used the term "Buddhist" and some of the real-world ramifications of these decisions, without picking sides.

Of course, I have shared my own viewpoints many times throughout this book—sometimes quite strongly—but you could say that, for the most part, I've been trying to provide an introduction to Buddhism that is descriptive overall, one that allows you to make your own judgments about what (if anything) about this tradition seems interesting or intriguing to you. At the end of the day, I believe that if someone finds claiming a Buddhist identity to be helpful in becoming a better person, then that's great. If not, then that's perfectly fine too. The most important thing to me is that we are cultivating wisdom and compassion, not what we call ourselves while we're doing it!

18

REFUGE

W here can you place your faith? Is there anything in your life that you can give yourself over to completely, with unwavering confidence and trust? Buddhists speak about taking refuge in the Three Jewels: the Buddha, Dharma, and sangha. These are the most important objects of faith and reverence in the tradition, the things that can always be counted upon, no matter what.

As you have no doubt come to expect, different groups of Buddhists have different interpretations of what the Three Jewels mean. In chapter 7, we covered the various interpretations of the word "Buddha," from an honorific term for a particularly wise man to an omniscient deity to the innate ability to Awaken that lies latent inside all of us. Others might say that the Jewel of the Buddha simply refers to Awakeness itself. We have also covered the Dharma extensively throughout this book, referring to the Buddha's body of teachings or to the whole extent of the Buddhist view. It is also used to describe seeing "reality as it is." Finally, we have talked about the sangha, the community of monastics, primarily in chapter 5. We'll get into some of the divergent interpretations of that term here in this chapter.

In many traditions, taking refuge in the Three Jewels refers to a specific ritual action that you perform as a commitment to Buddhism. For example, as part of the daily chanting exercises at the monastery where I lived in Thailand, we chanted, "I take refuge in the Buddha; I take refuge in the Dharma; I take refuge in the sangha." Repeat that sequence three times, and technically, you've now become Theravada Buddhist.

Taking refuge is also a way of speaking about having strong faith and clear understanding of what you can be sure of in your life. For committed Buddhists who believe we human beings are all living in a stormy sea of duhkha, the Three Jewels represent the only safe harbor. These are the only unshakeable sources of stability, the only things that can always be counted upon to provide strength and wisdom. This kind of faith is quite important for Buddhists of all kinds (although modern Secular Buddhists might resist the use of the term "faith" and prefer a word with fewer religious connotations, such as "confidence").

Traditionally, Buddhists express their faith in the Three Jewels by bowing to them. This occurs in various ritualized ways, depending on the local customs, and it might involve putting the palms together while standing, kneeling and touching one's head to the floor, or even prostrating oneself fully on the ground. Many Buddhists will bow to members of the sangha in the same way they do to a Buddha statue. Even if a monastic has been ordained for one day, by virtue of donning the robes, they become a representative of the Buddhist order, and laypeople no longer interact with them as individual personalities. Regardless of what kind of person they were just yesterday, they now represent the Jewel of the sangha. At least in theory, they are treated with utmost respect and reverence.

In their roles as members of the sangha, monastics provide important services in Buddhist communities, such as teaching and performing rituals and other religious functions. Monasteries serve as community centers and often represent the social hub of the village or neighborhood. This means that, despite the doctrinal separation between worldly and otherworldly pursuits we talked about in chapter 11, monastics always are involved in worldly affairs. They officiate at weddings, bless new businesses, and even hand out divinely inspired lucky lottery numbers. Their participation in these activities is totally normal across the Buddhist world.

Buddhist monastics have never been separable from the societies in which they live. From a historical standpoint, garnering support from laypeople has been absolutely critical for the success of the Buddhist order. After all, monks and nuns can exist only where there are enough donors with adequate economic resources to support them. Since people who have gone forth are supposed to abandon their worldly lives, including all money and possessions, they are in theory entirely dependent on the lay community for even their basic sustenance. Even the Buddha and his disciples subsisted by begging for food from townspeople. Establishing this symbiosis is challenging for temples located in places where the Buddhist lay community is not large enough or affluent enough to provide for the local monastics. I know many historical and contemporary examples in which temples have collapsed because the local Buddhist community was not large enough to support them.

On the other hand, some Buddhist temples are extraordinarily well supported by their local communities, to the point that they have become wealthy institutions. All over Asia, there are massive Buddhist complexes filled with gilded statues, jewel encrusted pagodas, and other ostentatious riches. While it may seem to go against the ideal of renunciation I explained in chapter 5, this accumulation of wealth by temples is justified by the belief that generously giving to Buddhist institutions is the best way for laypeople to demonstrate devotion to the Three Jewels. It honors the Buddha, helps to spread the Dharma, makes the sangha's life more comfortable, and increases donors' karmic merit.

From a Buddhish rather than Buddhist perspective, I think we can appreciate the important roles the sangha plays in local communities, while at the same time recognizing how this arrangement can lead to abuses of power. A cynic might even say that the whole setup is an abuse of power: First, Buddhist monastics promote a religious ideology that elevates them as an elite class with special access to

Awakening. And then they forward the doctrines of seeking refuge and karmic merit that convince the laity to financially support the temple.

I wouldn't necessarily disagree with that kind of analysis. But I would hasten to add that, in my own experience, the Buddhist organizations that have offered me the most resources, teachings, and opportunities for personal growth have asked for no financial remuneration whatsoever. I've probably spent, cumulatively, a full year of my life in meditation retreats and working or living at monasteries around the world. And throughout that time, I was never required to pay one dime (or one baht or one rupee). I have also seen firsthand how temples serve all kinds of refugees—whether providing facilities for homeless or mentally ill people, feeding stray cats and dogs, or even providing a sanctuary for birds in the heart of a busy city.

These experiences of mine contrast strongly with the commercialized spiritual scene that the author William Davies describes in his book *The Happiness Industry*. Mindfulness products alone produce over $1 billion per year, much of that from workshop fees, which range from hundreds to thousands of dollars per event. This arrangement seems totally backward to me. If Buddhism really is the one safe harbor in which I can take refuge from suffering, and you really are steeped in wisdom and compassion yourself, how on earth could you charge me exorbitant fees just to learn about it?

In any case, overcharging students for Buddhist teachings is a minor transgression when we look at the much worse abuses of power that can and do occur. Like all other religions, Buddhist abuses of power come in all flavors and sizes—from financial shenanigans to cultish behavior and everything in between. Too many "enlightened" Buddhist leaders have victimized vulnerable people instead of serving as reliable sources of refuge. And too many Buddhist organizations have been complicit in this kind of behavior for too long, producing untold amounts of suffering.

For example, since the #MeToo movement began in 2017, sexual abuses in Buddhist communities have been in the public eye. In fact, some high-profile Buddhist leaders have been accused of or charged with various types of sexual impropriety in recent years, including Sogyal Rinpoche, author of the popular book *The Tibetan Book of Living and Dying*; Sakyong Mipham Rinpoche, leader of the Shambhala International organization; and Pra Pawana Buddho, the abbot of the iconic Wat Samphran temple outside Bangkok, who received a sentence of 160 years in prison for raping nine underage girls living in the temple.

How can abuses of power, sexual or otherwise, be committed by Buddhist leaders—in particular, by major luminaries who are held up as models of Awakening? Of course, one possibility is that these individuals were simply deluding everyone into thinking that they were Awakened, when all along they were power-hungry sociopaths plotting to place themselves in the right position to manipulate people with impunity. I think this is unlikely to be true in most cases, but it's certainly a possibility we should consider.

Another possibility is that power and adulation can have a corrupting influence on even the most realized individuals. The typical rhetoric around high-profile Buddhist leaders presents them as perfect beings who can do no wrong. They are celebrated as paragons of wisdom and compassion, the epitome of human spiritual development. Followers who buy into this story become entranced by their teachers, worship them, idolize them, bow to them, take refuge in them, and hand over their agency and power to them. Perhaps being put in that kind of position is too much for anyone to handle, no matter how Awakened they are. Perhaps it's inevitable that these teachers will, despite themselves, come down with a severe case of "guru syndrome." They start believing their own hype, seeing themselves as perfect in every way and thinking they are free to do whatever they want to other people.

A third possibility I hear a lot of contemporary Western Buddhists discussing these days is that even the most profound and authentic Awakening may be insufficient to make someone a truly perfect human being. That is to say, no matter how deep your insight into "reality as it is," this realization does not automatically make you moral or compassionate or kind or caring—any more than it turns you into an overnight expert on nuclear physics, sculpture, or French history. Awakening may make someone suddenly feel that they are perfectly wise and have no more work to do on themselves, that there is no longer a need to face difficult emotional or personal issues. But an increasing number of Buddhists would say that this is simply untrue and would call this attitude "spiritual bypassing."

I think it is extremely difficult for celebrated teachers to avoid both guru syndrome and spiritual bypassing. The more celebrated they are, the greater the risk. Maybe this danger was on the Buddha's mind after his Awakening too. The myth of the Buddha's life relates that he was initially daunted by the thought of teaching and that he planned instead to hang out alone, remaining in bliss and ease for the rest of his life. As the story goes, he only agreed to become a teacher because the god Brahma (who in Buddhism is the highest spirit being in the pantheon but not an enlightened Buddha or bodhisattva) convinced him that some people only had "a little bit of dust in their eyes" and would benefit greatly from his teaching. I think that this story illustrates a great policy: only start your career as a spiritual teacher after you've received a personal invitation from the king of the gods.

All joking aside, Buddhist teachers give all kinds of arguments why putting your faith completely in a guru can be enormously helpful on the spiritual path. That might be true. But, personally, I have had an allergy to authority figures ever since my rebellious teenage years. For me, it all comes down to the flow of power—whether the teacher is empowering me or is drawing power from me. If "teacher" means facilitator, guide, and supporter, then I might consider that helpful. But if "teacher" means someone to whom I surrender my independence and judgment, then no thanks. If "teacher" means someone who is helping me to increase my skill in making my own choices, then maybe I'll give that person a chance. But if "teacher" means someone who I must bow to and idolize because of their attainments or superior knowledge, then see you later. While I respect everyone's right to create a group with a power structure that works for them, as long as their members are not being harmed, I see no reason that anyone needs to buy into a dysfunctional hierarchical teacher-student dynamic in order to learn about Buddhism.

Rather than take refuge in the monastic order or in a particular teacher, some practitioners are increasingly drawn to the idea of taking refuge in a community of equals, a development I think is a step in the right direction. It is now quite normal for modern Buddhists to use the term "sangha"—"community"—not to refer specifically to robe-wearing ordained monastics but more generally to communities of fellow practitioners. These days, many meditation groups are experimenting with nontraditional structures that emphasize flat hierarchies and power-sharing among their members. Some of these communities, such as the San Francisco Dharma Collective, have been explicitly designed to mitigate the abuses of power, spiritual bypassing, and guru syndrome I've described in this chapter.

I think this kind of power-sharing is also what the Vietnamese Zen teacher Thich Nhat Hanh was getting at in a famous speech he gave in 1993 called "The Next Buddha May Be a Sangha." Although he is a monk in a relatively traditional teacher role, his speech reversed conventional Buddhist ideas about power and respect in two important ways. First, he did away with the notion that a teacher needs to be a particularly powerful or perfect person by saying that the next Buddha may appear in the world in the form of a community instead of as an individual. Then he flipped the usual power dynamics on their head by taking refuge in his students instead of the other way around.

Still, for me, I think what resonates even more than taking refuge in a community of peers is taking refuge in myself as the sole judge of what is right for me. You might think I'm overly skeptical, but I'm on solid doctrinal ground with this idea. The Buddha is also said to have instructed his followers to rely only on themselves. On his deathbed, he is said to have told his disciples not to seek refuge in external teachers but instead to "be islands unto yourselves, refuges unto yourselves."

My favorite expression of this individualistic sentiment, however, was spoken by the ninth-century Chinese monk Linji Yixuan. His famously provocative words were: "If you meet the Buddha, kill the Buddha. If you meet the Patriarch, kill the Patriarch." Just to be clear, he doesn't literally mean that you should kill anyone. Linji is suggesting, in an intentionally colorful way, that we need to do away with our attachment to teachers. We need to find the Buddha or the Patriarch within ourselves, not in another person or in any other external thing. If we find ourselves idolizing someone else as a master, teacher, or guru, we need to kill that concept right away.

I do like the idea of taking refuge in myself. But, personally, I'd like to combine that with an idea put forth by Aaron Lee (1983–2017), the anonymous blogger behind *Angry Asian Buddhist*. That series of blogs, which ran from 2009 to 2016, tackled issues of race in American Buddhism while highlighting Asian American contributions. In his very last post, as he was battling terminal cancer, Lee offered a final reflection on what Buddhism had meant to him. In a refreshing reversal of the usual notion of refuge, he suggested that you should "be the refuge you wish to see in this world." Instead of seeking an object to place our trust in, that is, maybe we should ask ourselves how we can become more trustworthy for others. How can we become sources of strength for the weak or sources of security for the precarious? How can we ourselves become the safe harbor that provides refuge to all beings around us?

So, putting Linji's and Lee's ideas together, I'd like to forward the following as my own personal stance on refuge: "If you meet the refuge, kill the refuge . . . then be the refuge."

19

INTERCONNECTEDNESS

Did you hear the one about the Buddhist monk who visited a hotdog stand? He told the vendor, "Make me one with everything."

Sorry if you've heard that joke before, or one of its countless variations (sometimes it's the Dalai Lama ordering a pizza). Sure, it's corny, but it reflects a common perception that Buddhist teachings are all about "oneness," which I want to talk about in this chapter. If you ask me, I think "interconnectedness" captures a wider range of Buddhist ideas and perspectives than "oneness." But, in general terms, it's true that most schools of Buddhism see all objects and phenomena as inseparably interlinked. This oneness, interconnectedness, or interdependence of all things has been understood and described in many different ways by different Buddhist traditions and teachers—ranging from the philosophical to the mundane to the mystical—only some of which we'll be able to cover here.

DEPENDENT ORIGINATION

On the philosophical side, one foundational early Buddhist doctrine is that of "dependent origination" (also known as "dependent arising," in Sanskrit *pratityasamutpada*). This is a complex theory laying out a series of twelve steps or links of causes and effects. Taken together, this twelve-link chain is said to describe how karma works and how beings are continually reborn into samsara.

The crux is that, due to sentient beings' misunderstanding of the nature of suffering and their misperception of the world, they react to sensory objects with craving and aversion. This sets off a chain reaction, producing karma and generating rebirth, and the cycle repeats indefinitely until one becomes Awakened. The main takeaway from this theory is that nothing ever happens without an infinite chain of preexisting causes. You may not be able to understand all of the reasons why something occurs, but everything is always brought into being by a whole slew of previous conditions.

We might dwell on this interesting theory further and get into each of the twelve steps, but I feel like I have already spoken enough about philosophy, and I have mentioned that I'm not too fond of lists. So let's move on. . . .

VEGETARIANISM AND COMPASSION

Another common teaching on interconnectedness that is important for many schools of Buddhism is vegetarianism. Avoiding eating meat is a major part of East Asian Mahayana practice. In fact, I would say it's one of the defining factors in Buddhist identity in that part of the world. For example, I've known many people from Taiwan who claim you cannot be a real Buddhist if you eat meat. Meanwhile, for most of the Theravada Buddhists I know, the issue of being vegetarian doesn't even come up.

One of the main reasons East Asian Buddhists are so serious about vegetarianism is the notion that all sentient beings are intimately interconnected. Because all beings on the planet have been reborn so many times, they like to say, there is a good chance that the cow you are eating was your mother in a previous life or will be your child in the next. Since all of us are inextricably bound together by karma, the pain and suffering we cause by eating each other is simply abhorrent to many Mahayanists. Instead, they feel that we should take every opportunity to transform the intricate karmic bonds we have developed over countless lifetimes with each other into ones of kindness and compassion. (Even that truck driver who cut me off in traffic back in chapter 6: May they be well. May they be happy. I might have done the same to them—and worse—in previous lifetimes.)

It's not just Mahayanists who think about the transformational power of compassion. Remember the kindness I felt toward the mosquito after a summer of intensive contemplation on compassion at a Theravada Buddhist monastery? What is that if not a moment of interconnection between sentient beings, a momentary karmic bond between two links in an infinite chain of relations that has been ongoing for billions of years? One being was eating the other, and instead of killing it, the one being eaten responded with compassion. An infinite number of other relationships have taken place before and since—all of us loving, hating, helping, harming, feeding, eating, and affecting one another in countless ways. The act of compassion toward the mosquito may seem inconsequential from one perspective, but as part of this larger picture, that moment matters in ways that we cannot foresee or imagine.

Incidentally, although some Buddhists have argued that plants have Buddha-nature, they have not usually been counted in Buddhism as sentient beings, and they are not usually said to be reborn like humans, animals, gods, and spirits. Also, I should mention that there's no traditional doctrine on viruses and bacteria, since premodern Buddhists didn't know about them. My guess, however, is that most Buddhists would argue that microorganisms are not sentient, and I will say that I personally have never met a Buddhist who voiced an objection to developing a cure for coronavirus on the grounds of nonviolence toward microorganisms.

INTERBEING

For most Buddhists, it's not only all beings but also all objects that are intricately interconnected. The Vietnamese monk Thich Nhat Hanh calls this interrelatedness "interbeing." In an essay titled "What is

Interbeing?," he uses the example of a piece of paper to illustrate the idea. A piece of paper, he says, could not exist independently of all the other things with which it is connected. In order for the paper to arrive in your hand, we need the sun, clouds, rain, trees, loggers, paper mills, warehouses, stores, and everything else along the way. Each of those links in the chain, in turn, can't exist independently of all sorts of additional interconnected factors—the logger, for example, wouldn't exist if it wasn't for his parents and grandparents, or all the food he has eaten throughout his life.

There is an ancient Indian metaphor called Indra's net, or Brahma's net, that makes this same point in a more visual way. This vivid image is found in both the *Flower Ornament Scripture* and the *Brahma's Net Scripture*, two Mahayana texts that have been highly influential in East Asia. The metaphor hinges on the image of a massive net belonging to the god Indra or Brahma, which is made completely of jewels. The net extends infinitely in all directions so that it covers the entire cosmos, and the jewels are so clear and so bright that each one reflects all the others simultaneously. Thus, if you look at any one jewel, you see the reflection of the entire universe all at once.

Both the example of the paper and the metaphor of the jeweled net make the same point: Begin from any object, no matter how simple—whether a piece of paper, a cup of coffee, your own fingernail, or a discarded piece of trash on the side of the road—and follow the connections of interbeing outward. Before you know it, you'll realize that, in that seemingly mundane thing, you are looking at a reflection of the entire cosmos. All objects are inseparable from each other, and everything is constantly arising and existing together in one interconnected whole.

ENVIRONMENTAL AND COSMIC CONSCIOUSNESS

The interconnectedness of things means, of course, that humans are intricately unified with the environment. While we might think of ourselves as separate beings living "in" the environment, there is actually no boundary between us and our surroundings.

I mentioned in chapter 6 that in Buddhist philosophy both our bodies and the entire material universe are made up of the Four Great Elements. The earliest Buddhist scriptures describe how earth, water, fire, and wind—meaning the solid structures, liquids, heat, and movement—in the world surrounding us are constantly comingling with the same elements within our very bodies. We are constantly exchanging elements with the world outside through breathing, eating, drinking, and digesting. Even as our understanding of the physical world has developed significantly in modern times, this idea of our interconnection with the environment continues to be a central theme for Buddhist environmental activists in the present day.

This chain of connections also extends far beyond our own planet. We know, thanks to modern astronomy, that the elements that make up our material world were forged in stars that are light-years away. Premodern Buddhists also understood the universe to be impossibly large. Mahayana cosmology in particular posits an infinite number of worlds, strung across an infinitely long span of time. Each of us is just one of an infinite number of beings that are reborn an infinite number of times throughout this infinite world system. It would seem that any one individual's place in this vast cosmos would be so tiny as to be insignificant. Yet, if the universe is Brahma's net, then everything is a reflection of everything else. One's thoughts, intentions, and actions—no matter how small—can and do resonate far beyond one's own awareness. One word of wisdom or one small act of kindness reverberates throughout the entire interconnected cosmos.

MYSTICAL STATES OF ONENESS

Many Buddhists have also described a direct realization of the oneness of all things that arises in certain meditation states or is spontaneously realized in sudden Awakening. As we've discussed in chapter 8 and elsewhere, our awareness normally is filled with a kaleidoscopic swirl of sights, sounds, sensations, smells, tastes, and thoughts, all whirling around and around, nonstop all day long. This is what it's like to be us every waking moment. Most forms of Buddhist meditation involve training yourself to pick out one thing from that stream of phenomena and to concentrate on it. In mindfulness you focus on the breath, for example, and in meditation on the immeasurables you focus on words of kindness. But what if instead you looked at all of the phenomena that are unfolding in your awareness—everything—as one big fractal-like show?

These various phenomena normally seem distinct from one another as they arise, but they all have in common the fact that they are happening inside of my conscious experience. And no matter what is going on, I am never directly perceiving the real things "out there" in the world but rather am experiencing a construction put together by my own mind based on my sensory inputs. Seeing the common ground of all perceptions clearly reveals a kind of oneness to all phenomena. In Buddhist terms, you could say that the whole display of ever-present but ever-impermanent forms unfolding in my awareness—everything I sense, feel, think, or experience—is inherently united by virtue of sharing this quality of emptiness. Or, as the Tibetans say, everything we ever experience has the same "one taste" of emptiness.

Another kind of experience of oneness arises from seeing non-self clearly. So many of the thoughts that arise in my awareness have something to do with "me." For example, let's say I walk into a room, and I smell the scent of a mint plant. A thought might arise: "I'll make some tea with that later," or "I forgot to buy the ingredients to make mojitos at the grocery store." These self-referential thoughts also give rise to emotions. These may be complex, such as memories or fears associated with mint, or they may be as simple as "I like that smell." These kinds of thoughts and emotions construct and reinforce a sense of self, a sense that I am a person over here who has certain plans, ideas, and reactions to the mint over there.

But what happens when those kinds of thoughts don't arise? Is there still a sense of here and there? Throughout my waking life, my awareness is constantly taking in everything around me. Buddhist teachers often emphasize the importance of being in the moment or paying attention to your moment-by-moment experience. If we are actually attuned to what's happening in each moment, then we can see that whenever we experience anything—even if just for a split second before we start imagining we're a self who is experiencing it—our awareness is filled with just the experience itself. When there is no self, there is just the smell of the mint. Our experience is unified, not separated into the smell and the smeller.

Our appreciation for these brief moments of oneness—whether arrived at via emptiness or non-self—can grow through meditation, contemplation, and other types of practice. Eventually the moments may become more sustained as we come to feel increasingly unified and whole. It's also possible that we can become fully blown open to this realization instantaneously through a sudden Awakening.

The mystical experience of the oneness of everything is emphasized more in Mahayana forms of Buddhism than in Theravada, and particularly in Zen and Vajrayana. Having this kind of realization even for a moment can have a profound, irreversible, and liberating effect on how you perceive yourself and the world. You may discover a bottomless well of compassion that you can effortlessly share with all beings, because you see them all as inseparable from yourself. You may experience all things as interlinked entities and be overwhelmed with gratitude for how each one plays its own unique role within the grand unfolding of the universe. You may experience all things, including yourself, as a single field of experience that has no boundaries and is always transforming and giving birth to something new. You may be struck by the sheer beauty of nature or of everyday objects, seeing each as a miraculous expression of its own "suchness" (*tathata*) that couldn't ever be anything other than the way it perfectly exists right now. Some of the most mystical descriptions of this kind of realization say that the whole universe reveals itself to be the Dharma body of the Buddha. That is to say, the entire universe is experienced as one seamless, alive, wholeness that is Awakening itself.

The most profound experiences of oneness are beyond our ability to describe in words. When pressed for a description of the depths of his realization, the great enlightened hero of the *Instructions of Vi-malakirti*, for example, responds with a "thunderous silence," knowing that there is simply no way to do it justice.

～

Alas, I'm no Vimalakirti, and so this chapter has been filled with words. But, as always, I hope you will take them as an attempt to describe these perspectives neutrally and not to prescribe what you should think or do. Buddhist tradition has, over millennia, taught many different avenues and approaches to oneness, interconnection, or interdependence. These have included the concept of impermanence, the practice of mindfulness, the practice of meditation on non-self, and the realization of one's Buddha-nature. They have included teachings on karma, the middle way, and taking refuge. They have included the practices of skillful means, compassion, specific rituals, and philosophical inquiry. They have included the path of renunciation, the path of the bodhisattva, and even the path of not having any path. I am personally grateful to Buddhist tradition, despite all its flaws—and we've only discussed some of them in this book—for having invented and preserved this multiplicity of "Dharma gates."

Are all of these paths leading in the exact same direction? Maybe, maybe not. Most of them I have not walked, so I wouldn't know. Are all of these practices leading to true knowledge of "reality as it is"? Maybe, maybe not. I'm personally not sure we'll ever definitively know what "reality as it is" actually is! Will any of these ideas appeal to you personally? Maybe, maybe not. Now that you've learned something about them, it's up to you what—if anything—you decide to do with this information.

Whether you resonate with the philosophical model of dependent origination we talked about at the beginning of the chapter, the interbeing of all things, the infinite net of reflecting jewels, the one taste of enlightenment, or the Dharma body of Awakening is completely up to you. Only you can say whether or not there is anything of value here for your own life. Only you can make the choice to adopt the practices and to see for yourself if there is anything to them.

Just remember what the hotdog vendor said in part two of the joke:

> When the monk paid for his hotdog, the vendor kept all the money. "Hey, where's my change?" the monk complained.
>
> "Ah," said the vendor wisely, "change must come from within."

20

DOUBT

Whenever we go to a new city, my wife and I like to find one of those hop-on-hop-off tour buses and spend the first day getting the lay of the land. This both helps us to get oriented to the new space and gives us a sense of what we'd like to go back and explore further. I think of this book as a bit like one of those buses. Perhaps you've seen a few interesting sights on this brief tour of Buddhism that you'd like to investigate more closely. If so, throughout this book I've given you essential keywords, texts, and concepts that you can look up, and I've provided some further readings following this chapter. Unlike the typical hop-on-hop-off, we've also seen some of the city's less beautiful parts. Importantly, if you're interested in learning some of the practices I've described or in connecting with a Dharma teacher, remember the pitfalls I've cautioned you about that you might find along the way.

I want to thank you for joining me on this tour. But before we complete our journey, let's finish up by bringing our discussion full circle back to where we began: the story of the life of the Buddha. To me, one of the biggest takeaways from the myth of the Buddha's life is that we do not have to remain confined to the path set for us by our families, our communities, or our religious leaders. Siddhartha's decision to depart from the palace and enter the life of the spiritual seeker is only the beginning of his process of questioning authority. While practicing in the forest, he expresses doubt about the teachers he encounters, and he eventually abandons them all to forge his own path. Even after he becomes an Awakened teacher himself, the scriptures frequently depict the Buddha challenging religious authorities, schooling powerful kings and business leaders, and bucking conventional wisdom every step of the way.

In other words, the Buddha wasn't a Buddhist. He wasn't a pious follower of a preexisting religious tradition or spiritual program. He is called a Buddha precisely because he did not follow in the footsteps of someone else's teachings. By definition, a Buddha discovers the Path of Awakening for himself. The Buddha's example thus can suggest that we should question everything we think we know and be willing to set out for the farthest unexplored shores alone. The story of Siddhartha's life can provide a model for the seeker of spiritual wisdom that is premised on doubt, skepticism, experimentation, and individual responsibility.

A highly influential Pali scripture called the *Discourse to the Kalamas* (*Kalama Sutta*) gives an example of how, later on in his life, the Buddha is said to have taught his followers this same type of skepticism. In this text, the Buddha is questioned by the Kalama people as he passes through their village. They relate that they have been visited by many other religious teachers, each promoting their own positions and denigrating others. They ask the Buddha how to tell the difference between good and bad teachings. What criteria, they ask, should they use to evaluate the various options they have been exposed to?

The Buddha begins by validating their question, saying that it is right for them to be skeptical. He then advises them to use their own judgment instead of deferring to tradition, scripture, rumor, biases, the reputation of the speaker, or the fact that the speaker is their teacher. He advises them to accept a teaching only when they are certain that it is beneficial and wise and will lead to their happiness.

This warning is so important that the same refrain is repeated again and again throughout the *Discourse to the Kalamas.*

The tone here is markedly different than in most other religious texts, wouldn't you agree? Instead of prescribing a certain viewpoint, doctrine, or set of practices, the Buddha is clearly advocating free will, critical thinking, and impartial investigation. He is telling us to think for ourselves, not to be swayed by tradition, religious leaders, or other authorities.

Truth be told, there are many other Buddhist texts aside from this one that present the exact opposite message, impressing the importance of faith upon the reader. In fact, I would say that faith is a major theme in *most* Buddhist texts. In Theravada Buddhism, faith is counted as one of the Five Spiritual Faculties (*indriya*) that are considered basic prerequisites for making any progress at all on the Path (the others are persistence, mindfulness, concentration, and wisdom). In Mahayana, the message that you have to have unquestioning faith in Buddhist teachings is so strongly emphasized that it often comes with a threat of divine punishment if you do not comply. For example, the *Lotus Sutra*—a text that is particularly adamant in this regard—warns that anyone who criticizes the text or its devotees will be punished with leprosy and will be reborn with all sorts of deformities and ailments.

How can such diametrically opposed principles be taught by the same Buddha? If you think that the scriptures accurately represent the words of the historical founder, then this is a real conundrum that needs to be grappled with. On the other hand, as we discussed way back in chapter 1, scholars see these texts not as an accurate record of the words of a historical Buddha but as documents written down by different authors that represent the viewpoints of different traditions or communities of Buddhists. Scholars would say that the *Discourse to the Kalamas* and the *Lotus Sutra* represent records of what certain groups of Buddhists imagined their founder *would have said* rather than a verbatim report of the words of a historical person.

If you approach Buddhist texts from this more neutral vantage point, I think you'll agree that there's actually no reason they should be consistent with one another. Because Buddhist texts were written by many different people in different parts of the world over many centuries and because all of them placed different words in the mouth of the same founder, we would expect no less than for the same Buddha to say many contradictory things. Considering that at the end of the day we don't even have conclusive evidence that the Buddha was in fact a historical person—never mind evidence for what he did or didn't actually say—I think we have no choice but to use skepticism, doubt, and judgment when we approach his teachings.

Conflicting attitudes are not just expressed in different Buddhist texts but also in the daily lives of different Buddhist adherents. In my own studies and travels, I have encountered Buddhists who interpret the scriptures literally. I have met many who are engaged in proselytism, actively trying to convert people to their group or sect. And I have encountered many who are completely intolerant of those who do not agree with their own particular understanding of the Dharma. People who behave like this in the name of other religions are often labeled fundamentalist. Unfortunately, there is also a certain amount of Buddhist fundamentalism out there as well.

True story: I once had a job opportunity at a highly prestigious university canceled because of Buddhist fundamentalism. I was a finalist for the position, and, as part of my job interview, I gave a presentation that approached Buddhism from an objective, historical perspective. The faculty in the department loved it, and they were ready to offer me the position. But members of a local Buddhist community objected to my scholarly approach—calling the life story of the Buddha a myth, for example—because it didn't support their own fundamentalist understanding of Buddhist doctrine. In order to keep the peace with the local Buddhists, who had contributed significantly to the funding of various departmental activities, the department caved to the pressure and canceled the job search altogether.

While I have experienced things like that, I have also encountered just as many Buddhists who insist that "real" Buddhism is free from any kind of dogmatism. As we have discussed, many modern Buddhists see the Buddha as something like an early scientist or psychologist. These kinds of Buddhists like to cite the *Discourse to the Kalamas* text precisely because its skeptical stance squares well with contemporary notions of empiricism and free inquiry. Even while they are quoting the *Discourse to the Kalamas*, though, many of the most modern Secular Buddhists often still unquestioningly believe that the scriptures accurately describe how the mind works, and they are certain that Awakening is the inevitable result of practicing Buddhist techniques.

It's not my role to criticize people for holding whatever beliefs they so choose. However, my preference is to fully embrace the lessons taught in the *Discourse to the Kalamas* and to apply its message of skeptical doubt even to Buddhism itself. That is to say, I prefer not to take any teaching, teacher, scripture, or story at its word, no matter how widespread or popular it is. Instead, I prefer to evaluate these point by point, seeing what value each does or doesn't have for me as an individual. To be prescriptive for just one moment: I would likewise urge you to accept a practice or idea only after you have applied your own discernment and judgment, and only after you have verified that the practice or idea leads you toward what you are seeking. If you do decide to take up a particular Buddhist idea or practice, I think it's also essential that you ensure it does not become a type of fundamentalism.

There's a famous comparison of the Buddha's teachings to a raft that is introduced in the *Discourse on the Water-Snake Simile (Alagaddupama Sutta)*. This simile involves a man who constructs a raft from grasses, twigs, branches, and leaves, and uses this to cross over a large expanse of water. The Buddha asks whether, upon arriving at the other shore, the man should carry the raft around on top of his head. The correct answer, of course, is no: having arrived at the destination, the man should let go of the means of transportation that got him there. The implication of the simile, as I'm sure you've gathered, is that the Dharma is a vehicle to get you to Awakening and is not an ideology to cling to for its own sake.

I wanted to conclude this book with a chapter on doubt because this is the single most important message I want to get across about Buddhism. As I've said, I think there are many interesting ideas, beautiful teachings, and helpful techniques that have developed within the various Buddhist traditions around the world. This is a rich and diverse treasure-house of human culture that is very much worth exploring—although it would take many lifetimes to learn it all. However, I have no interest in encouraging anyone to become a faithful card-carrying Buddhist. I want to present the material and invite you to use your own faculties of discrimination and reason to determine what works for you.

~

Do we need to be Buddhist to derive benefit from Buddhist ideas? I think the Buddha from the *Discourse to the Kalamas* and the *Discourse on the Water-Snake Simile* would answer with an emphatic no. And I also think he would warn you not to carry this book around on top of your head after reading it. He would encourage you to approach everything that has been said here with a grain of salt and to investigate it for yourself.

Come to think of it, I bet the Buddha himself would tell you not to be Buddhist, but to be Buddhish!

KEY TERMS

AMITABHA: the Buddha of Infinite Light, who lives in a paradise far to the west of our world

AVALOKITESVARA: the Bodhisattva of Compassion, who hears the cries of anyone in distress and comes to their rescue

AWAKENING: the accomplishment of a Buddha and the goal of nearly all forms of Buddhism

BODHI TREE: the tree under which Siddhartha Gautama became Awakened; Latin name: *Ficus religiosa*

BODHISATTVA: a human being or deity who is on the Path toward becoming a Buddha, who devotes themself to helping all sentient beings

BODYMIND: the interconnectedness between the mental and physical aspects of a person

BUDDHA: an Awakened One who has discovered the ultimate truth and reached the pinnacle of perfection

BUDDHA-NATURE: the inherent Awakeness that's always there beneath or behind ordinary experience; also, the innate capacity to Awaken inherent in all sentient beings

BUDDHIST MODERNISM: modern interpretations of Buddhism that are compatible with modern science and psychology

DAOISM: a major religion in China that influenced Buddhism's development in East Asia

DHARMA: the teachings of the Buddha or, more generally, the ultimate truth of reality "as it is"

DHARMA BODY: the ultimate body of a Buddha, synonymous with all of reality or with Awakening itself

DUHKHA: the suffering, pain, distress, and dissatisfaction inherent to human life

EIGHTFOLD NOBLE PATH: the Buddha's prescription for overcoming the human condition and achieving Awakening

EMPTINESS: the ultimate truth that all things are mental constructs devoid of any independent reality

FORM: the conventional truth, or the ordinary way of seeing the world as composed of separate objects

FOUR NOBLE TRUTHS: the Buddha's four-part analysis of the inevitability of suffering, what causes it, and how to permanently vanquish it

GODS (DEVAS): high-level spiritual beings that Buddhism characterizes as powerful but not omnipotent

JATAKA: stories of the Buddha's previous lives

KARMA: both one's actions as well as their repercussions on one's future

MAHAYANA: the Great Vehicle; a diverse and inclusive school of Buddhism

MIDDLE WAY: a path between the extremes of ultimate and conventional truth (emptiness and form)

MINDFULNESS: a type of meditation where one remembers to focus one's attention on the processes of the mind and body from moment to moment

PATRIARCH: a member of the lineage of revered historical leaders of the Zen school

SAMSARA: the human condition of being trapped in endless rounds of rebirth into this world of suffering

SKILLFUL MEANS: activities that do not lead directly to Awakening but nevertheless forward the Dharma and help suffering beings

SUTRA: a Buddhist scripture written in the Sanskrit language

SUTTA: a Buddhist scripture written in the Pali language

TANTRA: a style of religious practice that involves yoga, breathing exercises, subtle energy practices, ritual cultivation of magic powers, secrecy, and non-dual imagery

THANGKA: a form of sacred painting common in Tibet and the Himalayan region

THERAVADA: Teachings of the Elders; the school of Buddhism most popular in Southeast Asia

TRIPITAKA: the Three Baskets; the Buddhist scriptural canon

VAJRAYANA: the Vajra Vehicle, Thunderbolt Vehicle, or Diamond Vehicle; the form of Buddhism most popular in Tibet and the Himalayan region, also practiced widely in Japan

VIPASSANA: insight meditation, or the investigation of how the bodymind works

ZEN: a form of Buddhism with a focus on meditation that originated in China but became predominant in Japan

ACKNOWLEDGMENTS

I am very grateful to the friends and family who read drafts of this book and helped me by proofreading, fact-checking, and giving general feedback and advice from academic and nonacademic perspectives. These include Nic Bommarito, Franz Metcalf, Marcie Salguero, Jeff Salguero, Ann Gleig, Cat Salguero, Alana Salguero, and Clement Pappas.

FURTHER READING

In addition to the books mentioned throughout the chapters above, these are some great starting points for more investigation of different facets of Buddhism.

SACRED TEXTS
- Access to Insight (http://www.AccesstoInsight.net). A freely accessible collection of English translations of most of the scriptures from the Theravada Buddhist tradition (including all of the Pali suttas mentioned in this book).
- BDK America (http://bdkamerica.org). A set of English translations of many Mahayana Buddhist scriptures (including *Vimalakirti Sutra*, *Lotus Sutra*, and others mentioned in this book), available for purchase and free PDF download.
- 84000 (http://84000.co). A nonprofit project dedicated to translating the Tibetan Buddhist canon into English and making it freely available online.

CONTEMPORARY BOOKS ABOUT BUDDHIST PRACTICE
- Pema Chodron, *When Things Fall Apart: Heart Advice for Difficult Times* (Boston: Shambhala, 1997). A classic book from one of the leading voices in contemporary Tibetan Buddhism, giving advice on dealing with adversity.

- Bhante Henepola Gunaratana, *Mindfulness in Plain English* (Somerville, MA: Wisdom, 2011). Another classic book, an introduction to meditation by a well-known Theravada monk.
- Sharon Salzberg, *Lovingkindness: The Revolutionary Art of Happiness* (Boston: Shambhala, 1997). The most influential introduction to Theravada-style compassion practice from another of the leading voices in contemporary American Buddhism.
- Henry Shukman, *One Blade of Grass: Finding the Old Road of the Heart* (Berkeley, CA: Counterpoint, 2019). A beautifully written account of Zen koan practice and the personal transformation one can experience.
- Thich Nhat Hanh, *The Miracle of Mindfulness: An Introduction to the Practice of Meditation* (Boston: Beacon Press, 1999). A hugely popular introduction to meditation, written by one of the most prominent Buddhist teachers of the twentieth century.

ACADEMIC AND CRITICAL WORKS

- Nicolas Bommarito, *Seeing Clearly: A Buddhist Guide to Life* (New York: Oxford University Press, 2020). The most readable and accessible introduction to Buddhist philosophy I know of.
- Pamela Ayo Yetunde and Cheryl A. Giles (eds.), *Black and Buddhist: What Buddhism Can Teach Us about Race, Resilience, Transformation, and Freedom* (Boulder, CO: Shambhala, 2020). Leading African American Buddhist teachers discuss issues of race, representation, and their vision for the future of the Dharma.
- Ann Gleig, *American Dharma: Buddhism beyond Modernity* (New Haven, CT: Yale University Press, 2019). An in-depth and intellectually challenging analysis of current trends in American Buddhism.
- Daniel Goleman and Richard J. Davidson, *Altered Traits: Science Reveals How Meditation Changes Your Mind, Brain, and Body* (New York: Avery, 2017). An overview of the current state of the science of meditation, by two of the chief scientists involved in the research.

- Chenxing Han, *Be the Refuge: Raising the Voices of Asian American Buddhists* (Berkeley, CA: North Atlantic Books, 2021). An analysis of the history of Asian American contributions to Buddhism in the United States.
- Donald W. Mitchell and Sarah H. Jacoby, *Buddhism: Introducing the Buddhist Experience* (New York: Oxford University Press, 2014). A textbook that I have used in my college classes to introduce the history and contemporary practice of Buddhism.
- C. Pierce Salguero, *A Global History of Buddhism and Medicine* (New York: Columbia University Press, 2021). A scholarly introduction to Buddhist ideas and practices about health and illness, and how these have changed over the past 2,500 years.
- Vanessa R. Sasson, *Yasodhara and the Buddha* (London: Bloomsbury Publishing, 2020). A mix of scholarship and fiction, the author rewrites the story of the Buddha from the perspective of the wife he abandoned.
- John S. Strong, *The Buddha: A Beginner's Guide* (Oxford: Oneworld Publications, 2009). A retelling of the Buddha's life based on scholarly analysis of historical and mythological materials.
- Evan Thompson, *Why I'm Not a Buddhist* (New Haven, CT: Yale University Press, 2020). An astute critique of modern Buddhism by a well-known philosopher.